FEMALE CRIME

The construction of women in criminology

NGAIRE NAFFINE

ALLEN & UNWIN
Sydney Wellington London Boston

First published in 1987
Allen & Unwin Australia Pty Ltd
An Unwin Hyman company
8 Napier Street, North Sydney, NSW 2060 Australia

Allen & Unwin New Zealand Limited
60 Cambridge Terrace, Wellington, New Zealand

Unwin Hyman Limited
37–39 Queen Elizabeth Street, London SEI 2QB England

Allen & Unwin Inc.
8 Winchester Place, Winchester, Mass 01890 USA

National Library of Australia
Cataloguing-in-Publication
Naffine, Ngaire.
Female crime : the construction of women in
criminology.

Bibliography.
Includes index.
ISBN 0 04 302004 6
ISBN 0 04 330393 5 (pbk)

1. Criminologists. 2. Female offenders. 3. Criminal
psychology. I. Title.
364

Set in 11/13 pt. Galliard by Vera-Reyes, Inc., Philippines
Printed in Hong Kong

Contents

	Acknowledgements	vi
	Preface	vii
1	The reasonable man	1
2	The frustrated offender	8
3	Learning crime	26
4	Masculinity theory	43
5	Conformity as control	64
6	Crime and stigma	76
7	The women's liberation thesis	89
8	Re-writing the human sciences: the impact of feminism	105
9	A feminist agenda for criminology	128
	Notes	134
	Bibliography	137
	Index	144

Acknowledgements

There are a number of people I need to thank. Paul Bourke steered me in the direction of feminist writers outside the discipline of criminology and encouraged me to explore the idea of 'the female voice'. In the early stages of the work, Allan Perry and Anne Edwards helped me with the organisation of ideas and material. Carol Bacchi offered many useful suggestions for developing the thesis and was a ready source of stimulation and enthusiasm. Duncan Chappell encouraged me to publish. During my visits to England, Carol Smart and Frances Heidensohn gave me advice. Some of the ideas in this book benefitted from an airing at the University of Warwick (1981) and Stanford University (1985). A Research Fellowship at the Flinders University of South Australia assisted me in the completion of this book. I am grateful to the editor of *The British Journal of Criminology* for permission to employ material from an article published in that journal. I owe thanks to Hilda Naffine who checked the manuscript. Finally, I thank Eric Richards for his many valuable comments.

Preface

This book is about criminologists and their view of women. The scope of the theories considered has been restricted to writing on the female offender from the late 1960s to the mid 1980s, although the need to trace the roots of these ideas has forced discussion as far back even as the 1930s. The reason for this restriction of focus is that the key figures in the criminology of women up to the late 1960s have already been examined in some detail by previous commentators, for instance, Carol Smart (1976). The essentially biological orientation of traditional thinking on the criminal woman of course has been identified and criticised at length in many well-known works. Further assessment of this body of theory would now be redundant. Consequently, this volume is a document of the 1980s.

To Hilda Naffine and Eric Richards

1

The reasonable man

Perhaps the least contentious proposition one can advance within the discipline of criminology is that women are more law-abiding than men. Official crime statistics and the unofficial data, derived from the admissions of undetected criminals, both reveal this to be the case. In the United States (Steffensmeier, 1980; Steffensmeier and Cobb, 1981; Smith and Visher, 1980), the United Kingdom (Smart, 1976, 1979; Box, 1983) and in Australia (Mukherjee, Jacobsen and Walker, 1981) the researches of criminologists consistently reveal the majority of the criminal population in almost every category of offending to be male. Virtually the only offence group in which women figure in anything like the numbers of men is petty property crime.[1] If one were to typify the average female offender, she would be a once-only shoplifter who tends to steal items of little value (Cameron, 1964; Brady and Mitchell, 1971; Naffin, 1983: Chapter 4).

At times it has been mooted that women are the recipients of chivalrous treatment by the agents of the law. The police and the judiciary have been thought unwilling to apply a criminal label to the 'fairer sex' which is, as a consequence, underrepresented in the criminal statistics (Adler, 1975; Price, 1977). This theory has been countered by research which has shown the sexes to be treated in a like manner when such factors as seriousness of offence and criminal record are taken into account (Green, 1961; Farrington and Morris, 1983). The

1

chivalry thesis has been further challenged by evidence of punitive police attitudes to certain types of criminal women—particularly those who are perceived to repudiate their femininity (Chesney-Lind, 1979; Parisi, 1982; Visher, 1983). The present understanding of the treatment of women by the processes of the law is that, even if women are the beneficiaries of 'chivalry' in relation to less serious offences (and this is now open to question), as soon as the offending becomes more serious or places their morality in question, they are likely to be dealt with more retributively than males who commit similar offences (Edwards, 1984).[2] The agents of the law are clearly inconsistent, even in their paternalism. Indeed, it is likely that official crime statistics are unreliable guides to both male and female crime. Varying degrees of 'chivalry' merely exacerbate the problem of interpretation (Chesney-Lind, 1979; Curran, 1983; Box, 1983:Chapter 5).

With more success, it has been suggested that recent trends in female offending constitute a new wave in crime. Women have been described as now substantially more violent (Adler, 1975) and more prone to engage in crimes against property (Simon, 1975). They have also been accused of invading criminal domains once exclusively male (Adler, 1975). After considerable debate[3] and scrutiny of statistics there is now general agreement that only one of these contentions is true (Smart, 1979; Steffensmeier and Steffensmeier, 1980; Steffensmeier and Cobb, 1981). Women's contribution to property crime, particularly of a petty nature, has indeed increased significantly over the past few decades (Steffensmeier, 1978, 1980, 1982; Smith and Visher, 1980; Mukherjee and Fitzgerald, 1981). Otherwise there has been little shift in patterns of the relative participation of women in crime.

This book is about the criminological endeavour to explain these statistics. It is a study of criminologists and their attitudes to women, rather than a study of criminal women and their patterns of offending. More particularly, this is an inquiry which employs explicitly a feminist perspective. It seeks to have women fairly represented in the criminological literature, to have their experiences rendered faithfully through rigorous scholarship. The argument to be advanced is that women should be accorded the same empathetic treatment that criminologists have so far reserved for their study of men. The demand is that women be allowed to give their own account of themselves, so that their criminal and conforming actions are invested with a greater sense of the sort of instrumentality and intelligence which criminologists have been willing to recognise only in the male.

The title of this chapter is drawn from the British law of negligence with its concept of 'the reasonable man'. Through the tort of negligence, British law recognises a range of relationships in which one party is said to owe another a duty of care. We all owe a general duty to other persons not to inflict harm by our foolish acts. There are also more specific duties of care. Shopkeepers, for example, owe a duty to their customers not to act in a negligent fashion through the sale of unwholesome products. Doctors owe a duty to their patients to exhibit a degree of skill usually associated with their profession. Likewise plumbers are expected to perform their services competently. The standard against which any individual's actions are judged is that of 'reasonableness'. The question asked is 'whether the defendant has acted as a reasonable man would have acted in the situation in which the defendant found himself?' (Baker, 1985:114).

In imposing a requirement that the defendant act reasonably, the law invokes what it calls an 'objective' standard. It asks, what would 'the reasonable man' do if he found himself in the same situation as the defendant? The 'reasonable man', however, is a legal abstraction. The standard of behaviour it invokes is considered impartial and impersonal 'in the sense that it eliminates the personal equation and is independent of the idiosyncracies of the particular person whose conduct is in question' (Rogers, 1984:95). The reasonable man is 'the man on the Clapham omnibus', according to Lord Bowen. Another jurist sees him as 'the man' who 'in the evening pushes the lawn mower in his shirt sleeves' (Rogers, 1984:46–47). In the case of the defendant who has professed to possess certain skills, he is also expected to be a 'reasonable man' who has the skills of his calling.

Law's 'reasonable man' provides a useful introduction to the argument of this book because he represents the male point of view. That is to say, the mythical man of law is intended to be ungendered, an objective standard of human conduct, and yet the characters used to illustrate the concept are invariably men. And, of course, they are deemed to be 'reasonable men'. In their search for a perfectly impartial standard of reasonable human behaviour, legal writers have retained in their mind's eye an image of a man, not a woman. The apparently generic reasonable man becomes unmistakably masculine as images are invoked of commuting civil servants and suburban husbands, 'in shirt sleeves', tending their gardens.

The point of law's 'reasonable man', for present purposes, is not simply that a male-dominated profession has, not surprisingly, invested a supposedly gender-neutral legal abstraction with male status. The point is also that the reasonable man of law is a fine example of an academic profession, finding its standards of ideal behaviour, or at least of 'reasonable' behaviour, in the male and not the female. When it comes to characterising the nature of being human, and in particular the better side of that nature, law has in common with other spheres of learning the practice of casting women outside the field of vision and invoking the experiences, the expectations and the values of the male. The result, it will be argued, is that when women are finally brought into the equation, they are regarded as in some way aberrant from the human = male norm. In law, the subliminal message is that reasonable people are men, not women. In other disciplines, the communication is more explicit: men are ideal and women are not.

This volume is about the male view which has dictated standards of acceptable human behaviour not only in law but across the social sciences. It entails the argument that criminologists are at one with their colleagues in associated fields of learning who have conceived the world through male eyes, but have presented it as ungendered social reality. The feminist task of this book is to expose the set of male values which has coloured perceptions of the sexes in the discipline of criminology.

The idea for this volume was stimulated by a paper published in 1975 by the American feminist sociologist, Marcia Millman (1975). 'She Did It All For Love' is a powerful feminist indictment of the treatment of women by sociologists of deviance.

The burden of Millman's argument is that her colleagues 'have come to associate women with the dullest, most oppressive aspects of society, or else to view their deviance in narrowly sex-stereotyped (and unappealing) terms, yet to see in our male deviants the expression of creativity and a courage to stand up to society's hypocrisies'. Millman observes also that the professional understanding of deviance has been constrained by what she describes as a 'systematically male-biased perspective' (Millman, 1975:253).

To demonstrate her point, Millman examined a small selection of criminological writings of the 1960s for their portrayal of the sexes. This confirmed that the sympathies of sociologists lay with their male subjects, who were consistently presented as more inventive, more interesting and more independent than the women who featured in their accounts of social behaviour. The overwhelming impression created by the sociological canon on deviance is that men alone are capable of standing up for their rights and defying convention, particularly when social rebellion is interpreted in terms of the 'heroic' qualities of bravery and loyalty to the oppressed. Deviant women, by contrast, are regarded as anaemic, as 'politically uninspired'.[4]

Millman's pioneering paper concentrated on a handful of paradigmatic cases of sexism in the sociology of deviance. In this volume, the brief is to consider all the major schools of modern social theory on the criminal woman.[5] The aim, in the first instance, is to identify in each school the dominant view of women. The larger task is to examine the way in which this perception has shaped theory and determined research outcomes. Exposing bias is useful but the more challenging project facing feminist scholars is to show how the employment of a male norm of behaviour, and the neglect of women, undermines much of the analysis.

Over the past decade, a vigorous feminist literature has evolved which throws into question the most fundamental categories of human thought. This volume is placed squarely within the context of this new feminist work. It is part of a common enterprise of feminists from different fields of scholarship who have begun to identify the sexist assumptions of their discipline. The project of these feminists is to uncover the masculine bias of knowledge. They seek to reveal that a male reality has constructed uneven accounts of the sexes. The male view, they say, takes the activities of men to set the standard from which all human behaviour is judged. It deems also that social experiences associated with the lives of men are valuable while the experiences of women are to be held in disdain. More fundamentally, the feminist endeavour has been to cast doubt on a good deal of orthodox theory about human nature and human behaviour which has been developed with such a slight or distorted knowledge of the female.

The proposition offered here is that criminologists have drawn on this discriminatory thinking disclosed in many of the older disciplines to construct their accounts of women. They have employed the very same unflattering images of women discovered by feminists inquiring into disciplines as diverse as mainstream moral philosophy and industrial sociology. Consistently, the male is portrayed as colourful, lively and appealing; the female by contrast is conceived as drab, inert and unattractive. Criminology's woman, in the main, has this considerable intellectual heritage.

The structure of the book is as follows. Chapters 2 to 7 deal critically with criminology and its treatment of women. Chapter 2 considers the postulate that crime is an expression of social strains of a mainly financial nature in the male and of an emotional kind in the female. Chapter 3 addresses the notion that offending is learned in social groups which approve of crime and from which women are excluded. The book next considers masculinity theory—the view that crime is symbolically masculine and is therefore an unsuitable activity for women. Chapter 5 examines the statement that crime is a natural and spontaneous pursuit whose curtailment depends on an acquired commitment to the conventional social order. Labelling theory—the contention that becoming a criminal is a matter of the application of stigmatising social labels—is the topic of Chapter 6. Finally, Chapter 7 discusses the impact of the women's liberation movement on the thinking of criminologists.

With an appreciation of the criminological female, the reader is then asked to consider the parallels between this unattractive character and her counterpart in other disciplines. The penultimate chapter points to the contribution of feminists in highlighting the misogyny of mainstream Western thinking and knowledge. Specifically, it looks at philosophy's idea of 'human nature', at psychology's interpretation of moral maturity, at political science's understanding of the political animal and at sociology's characterisation of the worker. Here is revealed the intellectual tradition from which criminology derives its conception of the sexes, a tradition which esteems men for their supposed autonomy, their intelligence and their force of character while disdaining women for their alleged weakness, their compliance and their passivity.

A program for a new feminist criminology is the subject of the final chapter. The closing message is that it is possible to draw a more positive construction of women from the material already collected by mainstream criminology. The stereotypes that have been imposed on the present body of findings derive from a male world-view which has distorted criminology's conclusions about women. A feminist re-examination of the existing research produces a different interpretation of woman which recognises her reason, her purpose and her essential humanity. The feminist agenda is to ensure that a balance is struck between the treatment of men and women in criminology. Once this work has been done, criminologists will need to return to their original task of uncovering the causes of crime.

2

The frustrated offender

The essence of strain theory, as the title suggests, is that criminality is caused by pressure or tension. The source of this tension is stimulated aspirations to achieve certain goals coupled with obstacles to their achievement. Frustrated individuals turn to crime either to release this tension or to achieve their goals via illegitimate avenues.

The progenitor of strain theory is the American social scientist Robert Merton (1949). Although he borrowed ideas and terminology from the French sociologist Emile Durkheim (1951), strain as the basis of a detailed typology of crime and deviance is largely his own invention. The key concept of strain, coined by Durkheim but adopted (and adapted almost beyond recognition) by Merton, is 'anomie'. Durkheim in fact had resurrected the term from the Greek word meaning 'without law'. He used it to denote the human condition flowing from those events which he observed in industrialising France: the disintegration of a widely accepted normative code which led to ungoverned aspirations and unregulated egoistic behaviour.

Although under the sway of Durkheim's thinking, Merton used the word 'anomie' in a quite different sense. To Merton anomie was not a state of normlessness which precipitated anti-social behaviour, but the condition experienced by individuals taught to want the goals of their culture but denied access to them. American society, according to Merton, was dominated by a concern for material wealth. The accepted means of achieving this monetary goal were education and then upward mobility through employment. Merton conceived the whole of (American) society as sharing this goal but not sharing equally the means of its achievement. Inequities in the social structure meant that the undereducated were limited in their occupational opportunities and were bound to feel frustrated by their disadvantages and consequently to turn to deviance.

Merton found support for his theory in the official crime statistics in which a disproportionate number of the poor and socially underprivileged was represented. He did not question the nature and meaning of the crime figures but took them to be evidence and proof of his theory of strain.

It was another American social scientist who took up Merton's idea of 'strain' explicitly to explain the different patterns of male and female crime, in particular the crimes of youth. In a landmark work, *Delinquent Boys* (1955), Albert Cohen interpreted strain as the main catalyst to the formation of delinquent gangs by male working-class American youth. Cohen suggested that the delinquencies of adolescent gangs were essentially a reaction to being judged and found wanting according to the standards of the middle class. In school, the working-class boy found himself equipped poorly for the routines of study and exams. He employed the wrong accent. An environment conducive to quiet learning was not provided at home. The prospects of satisfying employment seemed bleak and school an irrelevance. The boy's solution to failure at school and the accompanying sense of 'status frustration' was to invert the values of the middle class and construct an alternative culture.

In the delinquent gang, Cohen maintained, the working-class boy who was condemned by the school system thumbed his nose at conventional society. His life became a statement against the expectations and the aspirations of the middle-class child. In the gang, the lower-class boy embraced short-term hedonism and malicious and negative behaviour. Vandalism, joyriding and fighting all became means of expressing disdain for the colourless, hard-working and achieving life of the middle-class boy. In this manner the gang youth also sought to achieve status in the eyes of his gang peers. Anti-social activity demonstrated toughness and affirmed one's masculinity.

In the course of setting forth his theory of strain and the delinquent boy, Cohen provides us with a detailed picture of 'the American way of life'. To Cohen, the dominant middle-class culture in America is distinguished by a number of charac-teristics. Ambition is 'a virtue; its absence . . . a defect and sign of maladjustment'. There is an ethic of autonomy, of putting oneself first, of 'resourcefulness and self-reliance'. Altruism is almost a negative attribute. 'Although it recognises . . . a cer-tain virtue in generosity, [America] minimises the obligation to share with others, even with one's own kin, especially insofar as this obligation is likely to interfere with the achievement of one's own goals'. Altruism is a handicap to the full-blooded American. 'If one's first obligation is to help, spontaneously and unstintingly, friends and kinsmen in distress, a kind of minimum security is provided for all, but nobody is likely to get very far ahead of the game' (Cohen, 1955:88, 89).

Achievement is also a highly valued characteristic in American society, according to Cohen. In particular, 'there is a special emphasis on academic achievement and the acquisition of skills of potential economic and occupational value'. Rationality, too, is accorded a central place in the American value system, 'in the sense of the exercise of forethought, conscious plan-ning, the budgeting of time, and the allocation of resources in the most economic and technologically most efficient way' (Cohen, 1955:90).

American life, contends Cohen, demands also an ability to function well in relationships of a strictly superficial kind. The adult American 'circulates in a world of numerous transient and segmental but highly important secondary group relationships. A facility in such relationships, an ability to "make friends and influence people", or at least to avoid antagonising them is vital'. To conduct oneself effectively in the network of imper-sonal relationships which constitutes the life of the middle-class American, there is a need to cultivate 'self-control and the inhibition of spontaneity'. A further requisite of the successful American is a healthy respect for property. By this Cohen intends 'an emphasis on the *right* of the owner to do as he wishes with his belongings *versus* an emphasis on the *claims* of others who may stand in primary group relationships to the owner'. This collection of values and attitudes constitutes the core of 'the American way of life' in Cohen's view. It helps 'to motivate the behaviour which we most esteem as "typically American"' (Cohen, 1955:90, 137).

What is interesting about Cohen's conception of his society for the present endeavour to illuminate criminological depictions of the female is that Cohen regards his culture as gendered. Indeed Cohen is explicit in his recognition of an almost perfect fit between the valued characteristics of American culture and those of the successful middle-class male. He states unambiguously that his description of the standards of middle-class America is 'primarily applicable to the male role' (Cohen, 1955:88). His characterisation of what is valued in American culture, he says, is the *modus vivendi* of the successful male, not the female. Autonomy, rationality, ambition and restraint with one's emotions are the attributes of the person who makes it in America, but that person is male.

Although she is on the sidelines, the culture of the female is also present in Cohen's scheme of things. Moreover, Cohen shows no hesitation in presenting his own opinion of the female sphere. Women, to Cohen, are absorbed in a narrow set of relations with the opposite sex. This is the full extent of their interests.

> For the adolescent girl as well as for the adult woman, relationships with the opposite sex and those personal qualities which affect the ability to establish such relationships are central in importance. Dating, popularity with boys, pulchritude, 'charm', clothes and dancing are preoccupations so central and so obvious that it would be useless pedantry to attempt to document them.

It is no accident, according to Cohen, that 'boys collect stamps, girls collect boys' (Cohen, 1955:147, 142).

The message from Cohen is manifest. Men are the rational doers and achievers. They represent all that is instrumental and productive in American culture. Women's world is on the margins. Women exist to be the companions of men and that is their entire lot. The status of the female is contingent on that of the male: 'the female's station in society, the admiration, respect and property that she commands, depend to a much greater degree on the kinds of relationships she establishes with members of the opposite sex' (Cohen, 1955:141). While men proceed with their Olympian task of running all aspects of the nation, women perform their role of helpmate.

The style of personality which develops in the female cast in this role of emotional companion to the male entails all those traits antithetical to the dominant male culture. 'Indubitable femininity', to Cohen, is distinguished by 'ignorance, frailty and emotional instability'. Identifying ambition as a virtue, its absence a positive defect, a sign of maladjustment, Cohen with admirable consistency depicts the female as 'inactive', 'unambitious', 'uncreative' and 'lazy'. With the dubious virtue of altruism identified as a handicap to self-advancement, Cohen proceeds to talk of the female in terms of her 'affiliation, nurturance and harm avoidance', and with 'achievement' fixed as a central American virtue, Cohen depicts girls as wanting 'effort and acquisition of skills'. In short, the virtues that Cohen allows the female are exclusively those which he has deemed to be positively counterproductive in the American context. Females, in Cohen's account, are 'sociable' and 'timid'. They tend to affiliate rather than conduct their relations at the effective and efficient impersonal level of the male. Females 'nurture' rather than compete. They seek to avoid harm rather than placing their interests first. They are almost total failures, therefore, in the light of the 'get-ahead' philosophy of American society (Cohen, 1955:138, 143).

Cohen's evaluation of the prevailing cultural values of his country, of his sex and of women connect to a theory of offending in the following way. Despite the wholesale negativism said to characterise the male delinquent subculture, Cohen displays considerable sympathy for his male offender. From one man to another, Cohen seems to be saying, the delinquent boy still has a good deal to recommend him. Most importantly, he is unlike the female. The delinquencies of the gang member are almost to be celebrated as an affirmation of the masculinity of the dominant culture. As expressions of manhood, they are certainly more glamorous and colourful than anything associated with the female.

Male delinquency draws its palpable status from its association with the male middle-class culture, even though it represents an inversion of these values. Cohen explains: 'both the respectable middle class pattern and the delinquent response are characteristically masculine. Although they differ dramatically, to be sure, they have something in common. This common element is suggested by the words "achievement", "exploit", "aggressiveness", "daring", "active mastery", "pursuit"' (Cohen, 1955:139). Cohen does not stop here in his praise of the delinquent boy. 'The delinquent is the rogue male. His conduct may be viewed not only negatively, as a device for derogating the respectable culture; positively it may be viewed as the exploitation of modes of behaviour which are traditionally symbolical of untrammeled masculinity . . . which are not without a certain aura of glamour and romance' (Cohen, 1955:140).

If the trademarks of the delinquent male culture are its 'diversity' and 'versatility', the delinquent style of the female is the very antithesis. It is limited, unimaginative and usually takes the form of 'sex delinquency'. The girl who is unable to achieve satisfactory relationships through socially approved dating and then marriage will resort to promiscuity for its 'quick dividends' (Cohen, 1955:147) although it is ultimately a poor substitute. In Cohen's exposition, females do not commit the full range of offences because they are not subjected to the same pressures to perform as the male. Society's only expectation for the female is to marry well. It follows that it is only in the sexual sphere that the female expresses her successes and her failures.

Cohen's strain theory of female offending is never well developed. Cohen was interested in explaining the behaviour of the delinquent male and therefore focused on the stresses and strains of male life. When it came to the female, he assumed that the larger concerns of public life, such as work and money, did not impinge on the female psyche. In Cohen's assessment, girls are preoccupied with emotional matters. If strain is a precipitator of delinquency in girls, it comprises thwarted affections and therefore manifests itself in sexual transgressions. But even in this area of female specialisation, Cohen tell us, the delinquencies of girls pale in significance when compared with the behaviour of the male, were the latter only to be revealed. 'Were male participants in illicit heterosexual relations reported as frequently as their female partners, the richness and variety of male delinquency would be even more marked' (Cohen, 1955:46).

Neither the confidence nor the conviction with which Cohen presents his account of the different conventional and delinquent styles of males and females derives from a firm body of empirical data. Cohen assures his reader that it is 'useless pedantry' to endeavour to verify empirically his assessment of the male and female cultures. He informs us that his exposition of the different focal concerns of the sexes are 'so obvious' that it does not bear further discussion (Cohen, 1955:142).

Cohen developed his interpretation of the delinquencies of boys and girls in the fifties and therefore it might be said that his assumptions about the sexes reflected the wisdom of his day. The point to be developed in this chapter is that the emergence in the late 1960s of a feminist movement which has sought to question such wisdom has not led to the expected challenge to Cohen's style of thinking about women within criminological circles. The substantial influence of strain theory on the criminology of women of the sixties and seventies has not resulted in any real endeavour either to improve upon or to correct Cohen's formulation. While Cohen's depiction of a dominant monolithic middle-class American culture has fallen into disfavour in criminological approaches to the male (with cultural plurality or even conflict now assumed), in the literature on women it has yet to be seriously contradicted. Although there have been minor shifts of focus in the attempts of criminologists subsequently to employ and to verify his thesis, Cohen's account of the female offender remains firmly in place.

One reason, perhaps, for the wholesale acceptance of Cohen's view of strain and women was its consolidation in another influential text published five years later. In 1960, American sociologists Richard Cloward and Lloyd Ohlin presented a version of strain theory which essentially reaffirmed Cohen's position on the female. More particularly it restated the congruence between the dominant American culture and the culture of the male and put women on the margins of society. Women, it alleged, were peripheral to the central American enterprise of achieving material success and this was reflected in the extent and nature of their offending.

Cloward and Ohlin called their theory the 'differential opportunity' thesis. It entailed the claim that American society not only provides different opportunities for males from different classes to achieve material success, with the lower-class boy in the least privileged position, but it also provides different levels of accessibility to delinquent solutions. In this sphere of illegitimate competition, the boy from an organised criminal area is well ahead. He is provided with ample opportunities to engage in criminal activities.

The female, according to Cloward and Ohlin, is in the running for neither lawful nor criminal prizes. She is simply not a part of the struggle for material success. Along with Cohen, Cloward and Ohlin declare that the push to delinquency does not impinge on the female because it is the male 'who must go into the marketplace to seek employment, make a career for himself, and support a family' (Cloward and Ohlin, 1960:106). The delinquent subculture is therefore a male solution to an exclusively male problem. Females are neither pressured to achieve the major success goals of their society nor offered a delinquent outlet for their frustrations. The horizons of the female are confined to the family. The limited nature of their offending, its predominantly sexual nature, reflects this narrow set of concerns with personal relationships.

The work of Cloward and Ohlin also bears a strong kinship to that of Cohen in its affirmation of the attractive qualities of male delinquency. The boy who joins a fighting gang, for example, not only commands respect for his toughness from his peers and threatened adults—he also can expect to be 'admired' for his physical strength and his masculinity (Cloward and Ohlin, 1960:2, 4).

APPLICATION OF STRAIN THEORY TO WOMEN

The cultural objectives of boys and girls as defined by Cohen and Cloward and Ohlin were accepted, without question, by Ruth Morris in the mid-1960s when she shifted the focus of strain theory to the delinquent girl. Maintaining that blocked access to legitimate means of achieving culturally defined success goals precipitates delinquency, Morris hypothesised that 'obstacles to economic power status are more likely to lead to delinquency in boys, while obstacles to maintaining positive affective relationships are more likely to lead to delinquency in girls' (Morris, 1964:83).

Morris' was the first formulation of a strain theory specific to female crime. The main concern of Cohen, Cloward and Ohlin had been the delinquent boy. Their references to the delinquencies of girls were intended to throw light on the deviant behaviour of boys rather than provide any important insights into the nature of female offending. This notwithstanding, from *Delinquent Boys* and *Delinquency and Opportunity* it is still possible to glean the following theory about female delinquency: there is considerably less of it than male delinquency because girls are not subjected to the general financial pressures of the breadwinner; that which exists is mainly sexual because the goals of girls are narrowly relational; and girls avoid, and are excluded from, delinquent subcultures whose inherent violence is symbolically masculine. In the course of her research, Morris synthesised these ideas to develop a specific strain theory of female delinquency. This involved an analysis of the nature of the obstacles to feminine fulfilment and the consequent hypotheses that delinquent girls would tend to come from broken homes or families with many tensions, and would 'be rated low in personal appearance and in grooming skills' (Morris, 1964:83). Morris conceived female goals as slightly broader than those depicted by her predecessors. She believed that girls are not solely concerned with boys and the search for a husband. Theirs is a general interest in affective relationships, with family members and boyfriends as the focal points.

To test her predictions, Morris interviewed delinquent boys and their controls (56 quartets matched for class, intelligence and race) about their domestic circumstances. She also assessed their personal appearance and grooming. Generally, her findings were as expected. Delinquent girls came from broken homes more often than non-delinquent girls, while broken homes did not distinguish clearly the delinquent boys from their controls. Delinquents more than non-delinquents, and delinquent girls more than delinquent boys, rated their family's relationships as unhappy. Personal appearance, however, was found not to differentiate delinquent girls from their controls, although the delinquents displayed slightly poorer grooming.

Morris' pioneering research is less than satisfactory because it skims over important and interesting issues. As Cohen regarded it as 'useless pedantry' to document with any degree of specificity the preoccupations of girls, so Morris deems it unnecessary to consider whether delinquent girls suffer from 'significantly' worse 'relational' handicaps than delinquent boys. Instead she reasons that 'it seemed more appropriate to anticipate merely clearer differences between the female delinquents and non-delinquents than between the male groups' (Morris, 1964:89). This commonsense, rather than empirical, approach forms the basis of Morris' claim that 'the evidence is strong that girls are particularly susceptible to relational problems' (Morris, 1964:89). This is notwithstanding the finding that the tendency for non-delinquents to be more satisfied with their relationships with their parents is only 'somewhat clearer for girls than for boys', while the tendency for delinquents to be more poorly groomed than non-delinquents is likewise only 'somewhat clearer for the girls' groups than for the boys' groups'.

The tenacity of the idea that the failure of girls to succeed with boys precipitates delinquency is demonstrated by another American investigation which followed closely on Morris' footsteps. This time Harjit Sandhu and Donald Allen hypothesised that obstacles to 'acquiring, marrying, and retaining a husband' cause girls to turn to crime (Sandhu and Allen, 1969:107). The subjects of their inquiry were all female (there was no attempt to test whether delinquent males are equally disadvantaged in the marriage stakes) and comprised a group of institutionalised delinquents and a control group of high-school students. As well as a marriage-related obstacle index, questionnaire items included an anxiety scale and a measure of anomie.

In diametric opposition to the original hypothesis, 'the delinquent girls showed significantly less commitment to marital goals, expressed less desire to marry, and perceived fewer obstacles in the fulfilment of their marital goals as compared to non-delinquent girls' (Sandhu and Allen, 1969:109). Not surprisingly, delinquent girls were found to be more delinquent as well as more anxious and more anomic than the control group. In spite of the absence of any evidence that the delinquents' anxiety and anomie stemmed from concerns about marriage—indeed responses clearly indicated otherwise— Sandhu and Allen proceeded to maintain that their data provided partial support for their hypothesis. This support was derived in a curiously circuitous way. The members of the delinquent sample were said to be experiencing and suffering from obstacles to marriage attainment but blinding themselves to their plight: 'Psychologically speaking, they are using a mechanism of denial to maintain homeostasis' (Sandhu and Allen, 1969:110). More realistically, the authors conceded that their observations were equally consistent with the antithetical theory that female delinquency and obstacles to mate selection were unrelated.

A spate of self-report studies of the delinquencies of girls in the 1970s revealed that their criminality is not confined to sexual promiscuity but resembles the delinquency of boys in all aspects except frequency (see Introduction). Girls engage in the full range of offences proscribed by the criminal law, but they do so less often than boys. With this new understanding of female crime, strain theorists of the seventies found it less appropriate to characterise female delinquency as a product of 'relational' problems. They proceeded instead to test samples of delinquent girls for signs of frustration of a more general nature.

Female and male delinquents from a family court and a control group of school students were asked to consider their general opportunities in one American study (Datesman et al., 1975:107). Subjects were required to respond to such statements as 'I won't be able to finish high school because my family will want me to get a job' and 'I do/don't have opportunities that most teenagers have'. A stronger relationship was thus discovered between perceptions of blocked opportunities and delinquency in girls than in boys. In other words, strain was found to be a better predictor of delinquency in girls than in boys. Datesman concluded that 'girls who engage in delinquent conduct must perceive their opportunities as relatively circumscribed compared to other girls' (Datesman et al., 1975:116).

The test instrument employed by Datesman, with its focus on general life opportunity rather than the sort of narrow relational goals conceived for girls by Cohen, produced results more consistent with strain theory than those of Morris and Sandhu and Allen who were faithful to the original theory. It is surprising, therefore, that Datesman invokes Cohen's version of female strain for her analysis. Commenting on the ambiguity inherent in her opportunity index, that it was capable of more than one interpretation, she states that she had assumed *ab initio* that 'males were defining opportunity as the probability of success in work, while females were assessing their chances of achieving meaningful interpersonal goals' (Datesman et al., 1975:121). The perversity of this assumption becomes apparent after scrutiny of test items. This reveals that those statements which specifically relate to what have traditionally been conceived as male goals (that is, a good education and remunerative employment), are nevertheless better predictors of female than of male delinquency. When one also takes into account the absence of any 'relational' goals in the test instrument (it was originally designed for male subjects) a more obvious conclusion to draw from these findings is that girls are not preoccupied with family matters: they are at least as concerned as boys about their thwarted aspirations in the public world of education and work, and these concerns push them in the direction of delinquency.

The difficulty with such an interpretation of Datesman's data is that it poses another set of problems. Strain made sense as a theory of female conformity (or of the restriction of female delinquency to sexual promiscuity) when based on the premise that girls do not experience the stresses of the breadwinner. Thus it could be reasoned that girls are worried about neither performance at school nor employment prospects. Their entire concern is acquiring boyfriends and ultimately husbands. It follows that they are not subject to the same pressures to challenge the status quo as boys. Now if the empirical research discloses that girls are anxious about their occupational opportunities, or lack of them, strain should predict more female than male delinquency in view of labour statistics which consistently indicate the relatively poor employment opportunities of women. Most women tend to be employed in lower-paid, lower-skilled jobs than men, or not employed at all. But, as the statistics demonstrate, this does not cause women to be the principal offenders.

In a more recent inquiry, Douglas Smith considered the value of a number of social theories of criminality as predictors of female crime. The sample employed was considerable: nearly 2000 American citizens were asked to divulge their involvement in crime. In the course of his investigations, Smith tested the concept of strain by putting to subjects the non-sex-specific question of whether they 'personally have had enough opportunities in this country to reach [their] goals' (Smith, 1979:187). Responses revealed that strain conceived as perceptions of blocked opportunities was 'equally useful in accounting for estimated future probability of deviance for males and females' (Smith, 1979:191). What strain was unable to do, however, was explain the greater conformity of girls revealed by the survey. Although there was a similarity of correlation between self-reported delinquencies and perceptions of blocked opportunities for male and female subjects, when strain was held constant, the sex differential in offending failed to disappear.

Other research into strain as an indicator of female crime has focused on yet another set of goals and obstacles: what were conceived by the early strain theorists as the traditionally male pursuits of schooling and jobs. Over 1300 American high-school students of both sexes were the subjects of a study of the effects of strain on female offending conducted by Cernkovich and Giordano (1979). A self-report test of delinquency was administered to students together with scale items designed to measure 'awareness of blocked or limited access to legitimate educational and occupational opportunities' (Cernkovich and Giordano, 1979:147). Respondents were also asked whether they attributed any obstacles placed in the way of their success to sex discrimination (against females) and whether these injustices had triggered a delinquent response.

Although it was clear enough that girls' experiences of sex

discrimination bore no relationship to their offending, other results were less straightforward in their implications for strain theory. Unexpectedly race, rather than sex, determined the utility of strain as a predictor of delinquency. That is to say, blocked opportunities constituted a better predictor of delinquency among whites than among non-whites, regardless of the factor of sex. Even though, as the authors concede, these findings are difficult to interpret, they do indicate at least that strain is virtually as good at predicting female delinquency as it is at predicting delinquency in boys when the success goals in question are defined as educational and occupational.

Perceived access to educational and occupational opportunities also formed the basis of the measure of strain employed by Simons, Miller and Aigner (1980). In this case, the association between strain and delinquency was observed to be less significant for females than for males. Although female subjects were substantially more conformist than males, this did not reflect greater optimism about their opportunities, as strain theory would suggest. Instead 'the females in the sample were slightly less likely than the males to perceive that they would have sufficient opportunity to fulfil their occupational aspirations' (Simons, et al., 1980:48). Generally, findings provided little support for strain. Even though results were in the expected direction for males, strain was not a powerful predictor of their delinquency. In an effort to make sense of the greater conformity of girls given their greater pessimism, Simons and associates considered the possibility that girls are less concerned about their educational and occupational opportunities than boys. They also suggested an alternative interpretation of their findings, one which has already been offered by Cloward and Ohlin in their formulation of differential opportunity. This is that strain alone is insufficient to push an individual in a delinquent direction. There must also be opportunities to engage in 'illegitimate' enterprises. And as Cohen, Cloward and Ohlin all stress, the delinquent subculture is predominantly a male domain.

The few attempts to test the illegitimate opportunity hypothesis on female subjects have revealed that where girls are given the same chances to offend as boys, the nature of the offending of the two sexes is remarkably similar. Research into the nature and extent of the self-reported delinquencies of American school-children conducted by Joseph Weis indicated that although boys generally offend significantly more than girls, where the delinquency is a 'sex-shared activity'—such as violating curfew, getting drunk and smoking marijuana—the percentage of male and female offenders is roughly the same (Weis, 1976:28). Similarly, a study of the self-reported delinquencies of English school-children suggests that opportunity is an important variable in the offending of girls. The British criminologist Robert Mawby asked his subjects to describe their play activities and found that the girls had fewer opportunities to offend than the boys. Girls were 'significantly more likely to "play or muck about" in the home, and boys more likely "to play or muck about" on deserted land' (Mawby, 1980:540). Mawby also discovered that, notwithstanding the overall greater frequency of male offending, when girls were in a similar position to offend as boys they tended to be as delinquent. This was evident from the disclosure that in those situations where girls were most likely to be found, that is, at school and in the home, girls were as likely to commit thefts as boys. By contrast, the more marked differences between the offending of girls and boys related to those offences associated with the male-dominated outdoor play activities. Mawby surmised that the greater conformity of girls was perhaps a consequence of their more circumscribed play activities out of school.

Considered as a single body of data, the evidence yielded by the various researchers into strain fails to coalesce into a clear and consistent picture of the female offender. For those authors who regarded strain for girls as blocked access to relational goals, findings certainly conflict. While Morris observed that delinquent girls perceived obstacles to these goals as 'somewhat' worse than non-delinquent girls and boys, Sandhu and Allen found that their delinquent girls were actually less worried about prospects for marriage, and saw fewer obstacles to its achievement, than non-delinquents. When female goals were defined in a gender-neutral way (that is, 'your goals'), strain proved to be a better predictor of female delinquency than of the offending of

boys (for Datesman) and as good a predictor of female delinquency (for Smith), although it was an insufficient explanation
of the greater conformity of girls. Those researchers who
tested girls for what have traditionally been defined as male
goals—work and education—discovered that race rather than
sex determined the efficacy of the theory (Cernkovich and
Giordano) and that strain was a worse predictor of delinquency
in girls than in boys (Simons, et al.).

The research which has produced the most straightforward
and helpful findings for strain theory was not designed specifically to test this theory but instead addressed the issue of
opportunities to offend. Although it is arguable that opportunity theory is more appropriately considered in a discussion of
differential association, the subject of the next chapter, it was
adopted by the strain theorists Cloward and Ohlin as an integral
part of their thesis of differential opportunity. Research into
the delinquent opportunities of girls reveals that their offending
is remarkably similar to that of boys in those locales where girls
congregate as much as boys—that is, the school and the
home—and in those situations where social activities are
mixed.

The weight of evidence produced by researchers into strain
has probably tended more to contradict than to confirm Cohen's formulation. There is little here to justify the claim that
the sexes react differently to impeded goals or indeed that their
aims do not correspond. Theorists are therefore perverse in
their belief that women's behaviour is more uniform and conventional than men's because women are not subjected to the
stresses of the male role. They ignore the evidence when they
insist that women are insulated from the pressures of public
life, that their role is less demanding than the male role and that
they thus do not experience pressures causing them to deviate.

The principal disclosure of this review of the work on strain
and women is that criminologists, from the fifties to the present, have operated with a flawed theory and, not surprisingly,
the result has been confusion. Evident throughout the literature is a persistent but misguided loyalty to strain theory's
original expositor and his sexist assumptions. Albert Cohen
based his interpretation of male and female behaviour on a set

of propositions which maintained the value of male activity, be it law-abiding or criminal, and the unimportance of female action. Cohen assumed a substantial similarity between the dominant culture of American society and that of the American male. He believed that the delinquent boy also imbibed the American male value system, although his behaviour was a partial inversion of these standards. And Cohen tacitly endorsed the masculinity of his nation, of his sex, and more particularly of the delinquent boy—the romantic and glamorous 'rogue male'.

The female, in Cohen's scheme, was cast in the role of 'other'. Her position was not only unattractive but, in the eyes of many a male, contemptible. The female was on the margins of the American culture. Her lawful and delinquent pursuits were inevitably then a reflection of her exclusive concern with the opposite sex. Accordingly they lacked the daring, the interest and the sheer appeal of male crime and conformity.

The conceptual flaw in the research into strain since the 1950s entails the almost total failure of criminologists to examine critically Cohen's original assumptions about men and women. The need to do so has been manifest from the earliest tests of strain which have yielded unexpected results. The depiction of the female as fully absorbed in romantic relationships has proven unhelpful: it does not appear to be a credible explanation of the actions of women. And yet criminologists continue to operate substantially from Cohen's premises, regardless. Modifications of test instruments to extend the range of frustrations to which women might be susceptible (such as that of Datesman) have not been accompanied by the necessary revision of, or challenge to, the original version of the theory. While criminologists have come to view it as appropriate to test females for frustrations once thought to vex only the male, and have even recognised that girls do care about their employment prospects, they have not done the additional work of rethinking the core theory which assumed that such general concerns were irrelevant to the 'other' sex. They certainly have not endeavoured to discover how women themselves define their goals and interests—whether they centre on family matters or extend into the public arena as traditionally defined.

Cohen's view of the sexes and society remains substantially

intact. The 'strain' theory of female offending continues to emphasise its triviality and its close relation to the narrow range of concerns or anxieties generated by the female role. Female offending is trifling because nothing of public significance is demanded of women. Their criminality is seen to be narrow in scope because females have only one priority: achieving success with males.

3

Learning crime

The theory of differential association when applied to women may be stated simply. Women do not mix in criminal circles. Their gender role defines them as wives and mothers and restricts their sphere of influence and experience to the home. As a consequence, women and girls do not roam the streets learning to fight and steal. They do not enter organised crime by acquiring the skills of those who have already infiltrated criminal subcultures; women's involvement in crime is considerably less than that of men who have entry into the criminal underworld. In the words of the Australian criminologist Jocelynne Scutt,

> the female, because of her isolated position in the household . . . is in no position to acquire attitudes accepting of criminal mores—or is not in such an advantageous position as is the male. The sphere in which the male moves in current Western society is so much wider than that of the female, that his opportunities in contact with both social and anti-social standards and activities are considerably greater (Scutt, 1978a:10–11).

The idea that criminality is normal, learned behaviour goes back to 1939 when Edwin Sutherland introduced the theory in *Principles of Criminology* (although an historian might want to argue that it goes back further still—to the eighteenth century and the notion of the 'dangerous classes'). Over a number of revisions of his text in collaboration with Donald Cressey, Sutherland crystallised his theory of 'differential association' into nine propositions which together explained the process by which a person comes to engage in crime (Sutherland and Cressey, 1966).

First, 'criminal behaviour is learned'. The notion that criminality is innate or inherited is repudiated. A person does not knowingly engage in crime without some training.

Second, 'criminal behaviour is learned in interaction with other persons in a process of communication'. This communication is both verbal and non-verbal: it includes gestures.

Third, 'the principal part of the learning of criminal behaviour occurs within intimate personal groups'. The mass media play only a small part in transmitting messages which induce criminal behaviour.

Fourth, 'when criminal behaviour is learned, the learning includes: (a) techniques of committing the crime, which are sometimes very complicated, sometimes very simple; (b) the specific direction of motives, drives, rationalisations, and attitudes'.

Fifth, 'the specific direction of motives and drives is learned from definitions of the legal codes as favourable or unfavourable'. Sutherland saw American society as culturally mixed and therefore harbouring both criminal and law-abiding attitudes.

Sixth, 'a person becomes a delinquent because of an excess of definitions favourable to violation of law over definitions unfavourable to violation of law'. This is the essence of differential association. Isolation from law-abiding influences or mores and exposure to those who endorse criminality lead to an individual becoming criminal.

Seventh, 'differential associations may vary in frequency, duration, priority, and intensity'. For example, associations with criminal parents will have greater effect than the criminality of a passing acquaintance.

Eighth, 'the processes of learning criminal behaviour by association with criminal and anti-criminal patterns involves all the mechanisms that are involved in any other learning'.

Finally, ninth, 'while criminal behaviour is an expression of general needs and values, it is not explained by those general needs and values, since non-criminal behaviour is an expression of the same needs and values'. Sutherland saw what were usually supposed to be criminal motives, such as economic need, as explaining both criminal and law-abiding behaviour. These motives therefore did not differentiate the offender from the non-offender. What did was exposure to criminal influences, the availability of which was dependent on the individual's location in society.

Sutherland's theory of differential association, the theory of the transmission and learning of criminal patterns, extends beyond the simple learning processes of criminal motives. It is embedded in a more general critique of post-industrial societies. Sutherland's broader concern is to explain the presence of both criminal and non-criminal cultural patterns in modern society. The co-existence of these patterns Sutherland describes as a state of 'normative conflict'.

There are strong parallels between Sutherland and Cohen's appraisal of modern America. Both depict contemporary Western culture in terms of a cult of the individual. They describe a society which places a premium on competition, achievement and the pursuit of material gain, but denies its members equal access to its goals. Sutherland and Cohen diverge, however, on several points. Whereas Cohen stresses the homogeneity of the norms of American society, believing that the goals of the middle-class male are common to all, Sutherland insists on a 'heterogeneity of norms' (Sutherland and Cressey, 1966:103). Sutherland agrees with the point that Western society esteems 'individual enterprise' and 'economic competition', but suggests that there is a diversity of views about the appropriate ways of making money. Individuals who find lawful channels to financial rewards blocked are likely to develop alternative and illegal cultural means of pursuing their interests. Sutherland concurs with Cohen that one response to frustrated economic goals is the nihilistic delinquent gang, but maintains that there is also a variety of other reactions. Organised criminal subcultures, for example, can develop at all social levels to expedite the process of getting rich. Crime, says Sutherland, is not exclusively the province of frustrated working-class youth who find themselves consigned to the bottom of the social heap. Rather, it is endemic to advanced societies, an integral feature of the lives of people of all social standings. It is a result of a desire for personal advancement, as well as the weakened moral basis of the legal system. The cult of the individual, according to Sutherland, has attenuated the moral grip of the law and fostered the development of a questioning attitude to the value of being law-abiding. Whereas Cohen depicts a moral consensus around the values of the middle class, Sutherland observes a state of moral conflict. He describes a hedonistic and egoistic society in which there are shifting positions on the wrongfulness of unlawful gain.

Another point of divergence between the theories of Cohen and Sutherland entails their evaluations of the American way of life. Cohen at least tacitly applauds the ethic of competition and self-advancement. Sutherland seems to condemn it. According to Sutherland,

> individualism is not a positive principle of social organisation . . .
> The ideology of individualism has encouraged the individual to disregard social welfare in the interest of his selfish satisfactions . . .
> Public welfare need not be considered for it will be best realised if each person works for his own selfish interests (Sutherland and Cressey, 1966:104).

Modern industrial societies, to Sutherland, are distinguished by a dearth of social responsibility, a tendency to advance the self at the expense of others. Such societies embrace a plurality of values about the most appropriate means to self-advancement, lawful or otherwise, because there is no common endeavour to support and protect a community of cherished persons. The individual comes before community. Sutherland cites Veblen approvingly: 'The ideal pecuniary man is like the ideal delinquent in his unscrupulous conversion of goods and persons to his own ends, and in a callous disregard of the feelings and wishes of others' (Sutherland and Cressey, 1966:104).

There is a further discrepancy between the theories of Cohen and Sutherland. Cohen is explicit in his depiction of American life as masculine; it is a culture from which women are excluded. Cohen also makes plain that his interest is in male behaviour. His theory of the formation of delinquent gangs is a sex-specific explanation of the criminality of the working-class boy. Sutherland, on the other hand, maintains that his theories of crime and society are general in their application. From the outset, he declares that 'the objective of criminology is the development of a body of general and verified principles'. Unlike Cohen, in his description of modern society, Sutherland fails to allude to the cultural hegemony of the male. He observes that 'each person' is expected 'to pursue his private ends in the most efficient manner possible'. Sutherland's account of crime is presented as a general (non-sex-specific) theory of modern human behaviour based on a general theory of modern society (Sutherland and Cressey, 1966:3, 104).

Juxtaposition of the work of Cohen and Sutherland thus produces a number of important distinctions. Cohen appears to endorse self-interested masculinity as an American mode. Sutherland repudiates this modern value of egoism, preferring altruism. Cohen sees a homogeneous society bound together by the standards of the middle-class. Sutherland depicts cultural diversity, a concomitant of the lack of social cohesion, of community solidarity. Cohen offers an account of sex-specific patterns of offending. Sutherland professes a larger achievement. His is a general theory limited in scope by neither class nor sex.

There comes a point in one's reading of Sutherland when one's suspicions are aroused about his claim to be gender-neutral. This point is late in his volume, however, page 138 to be precise. Here one finds Sutherland's first specific references to the female. And with them one begins to doubt both the generality and the non-gendered nature of all his preceding statements. Sutherland deals with the female in a small section of a chapter on physiology and crime. Here he concedes that 'sex status is of greater statistical significance in differentiating criminals from non-criminals than other traits' (Sutherland and Cressey, 1966:138). The male crime rate is 'greatly in excess' of the crime rate for women. How does Sutherland explain this peculiar constant in the crime patterns in the light of his non-gendered theory of cultural variation and 'normative conflict'?

It is in the course of reading Sutherland's brief account of the greater conformity of the female that one begins to form a clear impression that women have been entirely eclipsed from Sutherland's vision of modern America, with its diversity of values generated by a preference for individualism. One learns, in a single extended paragraph, that females do not fit Sutherland's model. They are neither diverse nor individualistic. Indeed their chief characteristic is their cultural homogeneity, their common socialisation into a single role which demands of them attributes antithetical to those which have value in the larger society. 'From infancy, girls are taught that they must be nice, while boys are taught that they must be rough and tough; a boy who approaches the behaviour of girls is regarded as a "sissy" (Sutherland and Cressey, 1966:142). Females do not have the freedom of males, according to Sutherland. They are not only 'supervised more carefully'; they are also positively schooled in what Sutherland terms 'anti-criminal behaviour patterns' (Sutherland and Cressey, 1966:142). The analysis of female conformity develops no further than this. Female behaviour and the female experience simply appear as significant exceptions to the central activity and ethic of modern society. Femaleness emerges as an anomaly. Female homogeneity contrasts with the diversity of the general culture. Female altruism or 'being nice' contrasts with egoism. The constraints of the female experience contrast with the limitless pursuit of gain of the rest of society.

Sutherland's treatment of the female undermines and indicts his self-professed generality. Sutherland is neither general nor gender-neutral in his depiction of crime and society. He describes as general what he later reveals to be limited to the male case. Although he appears to abhor the ethic of the individual, Sutherland is nevertheless sensitive to the cachet which attaches to material achievement, through whatever means. It is only later that we learn that this cachet is reserved for the male and that the ethic of altruism, lauded earlier in the text, is seen to be shameful when it appears in a much-diluted form, 'niceness', in association with the female.

The criminological theory offered by Sutherland to explain the different behaviour of the sexes entails the simple claim that whenever the individual is female, cultural diversity is extinguished and anti-criminal patterns are fostered. Freedom of movement is also curtailed when the subject is female. When the individual is male, a wide range of criminal and anti-criminal patterns are available for learning. The male is encouraged to absorb the individualism and competitive ethic underpinning this cultural plurality. The result is greater variation in male behaviour, including criminality. The greater uniformity and conventionality of the female is a logical outcome of a cloistered existence in which any activity not directly related to the domestic role is discouraged.

In the following review of efforts within the criminology of women to test the theory of differential association it will be revealed that Sutherland's original formulation remains unmodified and unchallenged. The notion that constraints on the experience of the female limit her offending, while males are let free to engage in a range of behaviour, seems now to be generally accepted to the point of assuming the status of received wisdom. The tendency of criminologists since Sutherland to focus on the exclusion of females from criminal subcultures, rather than the fostering of law-abiding patterns in the female, has served to heighten the impression that women are to be understood in terms of their disbarment from the dominant (male) culture. The female lot, in this literature, is conceived as a state of negativity, of 'otherness'. Women are kept outside all the cultures of the male, criminal and otherwise. The only place women positively belong is in the family.

LEARNING THEORY AND WOMEN

The first explicit application of differential association to females was by Ruth Morris in her effort to explain female conformity. She hypothesised that 'there is a relative absence of a deviant subculture for female delinquents, and absence of subcultural as well as cultural support for female delinquency' (Morris, 1965:251). To test her thesis, Morris looked for evidence of greater social disapproval of female than of male delinquency as well as the manifestation of greater shame in female delinquents than in boys who offended. Her evidence was derived from samples of male and female delinquents and non-delinquents (56 quartets) living in an American industrial city, Flint, Michigan, who were matched for social class, intelligence, age and grade in school. The idea behind her investigation was that '[as] Sutherland maintains . . . an individual will become delinquent when attitudes among his intimate friends favouring delinquent behaviour outweigh those opposing it'. Both delinquent and non-delinquent subjects were asked how they 'would feel toward their best friends if these friends had committed specific delinquent acts . . . how they thought most of their friends would feel toward them if they themselves were to commit these delinquencies . . . [and] to estimate what proportion of their friends actually had committed each of the typical delinquent offences included' (Morris, 1965:251–2).

The delinquent acts which Morris listed in her questionnaire, however, were not identical for males and females. Like other criminologists at the time of writing, Morris believed that female delinquency was primarily sexual. Accordingly, where males were asked about motor vehicle thefts and assaults, females were asked about 'heavy petting' and sexual promiscuity. Other items such as 'truancy' and 'running away from home' were administered to both male and female subjects. As a further indicator of shame felt about delinquencies, all subjects were asked to divulge any contacts with the police.

In general terms, Morris' findings confirmed her hypothesis. Delinquent girls were more hesitant to report their delinquencies than delinquent boys, while non-delinquent boys were significantly more likely to admit to police contacts than non-delinquent girls. Boys were more tolerant of male delinquency than of female delinquency, while girls were more critical of delinquency in general than were boys. Girls were not, however, more critical than boys of delinquency in girls. Boys, and delinquents as a group, believed their friends to be more tolerant of delinquency than did non-delinquents and girls. Delinquents were observed to have more delinquent friends than non-delinquents. And although delinquents were found generally to commit offences with others of the same sex (boys failing to know more delinquent girls than did female subjects), non-delinquent boys had more delinquent friends of both sexes than did non-delinquent girls.

From these findings, Morris concluded that 'non-delinquents live in a social atmosphere with fewer cultural and subcultural supports for delinquency', as Sutherland's differential association predicts. The sex differential in crime was also, according to Morris, at least partly explained by differential association. She noted that 'all girls, delinquents and non-delinquents, are continuously faced with a relative absence of subcultural support for delinquency and a much more stringent social disapproval of delinquency than are boys' (Morris, 1965:265).

A somewhat different approach to gender role and differential association was adopted by Shirley Merrit Clark (1964) in her investigation into the offending of American, institutionalised, delinquent boys and girls in 1960 and 1961. Like Morris, Clark was concerned to explain the more 'restricted focus' of female delinquency (which she, too, believed to be essentially sexual) by the paucity of delinquent companions for girls. Her hypotheses were that 'female delinquency will be less extensive than male delinquency' and that the 'association between delinquency onset and companionship will be less for female delinquents than male delinquents' (Clark, 1964:218).

Clark's findings failed to support either hypothesis. Consistent with the results of later self-report studies,[1] she found a 'strikingly similar pattern' in the frequency of male and female delinquency. This led her to conclude that 'the extensity of female delinquency is much greater than previously supposed and the difference between male and female extensity is evidently not great' (Clark, 1964:220). And instead of the delinquencies of girls being unrelated to their type of companions, Clark discovered that 'companionship seems to be as much a part of the delinquent act for girls as for boys' (Clark, 1964:224).

Although Clark's findings were not as she expected, they nevertheless point to the value of differential association as an indicator of female criminality. Instead of the greater conformity of girls being attributed to a dearth of delinquent companions (Clark's complex hypothesis), the female subjects are found to be similar to boys in the amount of their delinquency and also, like boys, they are connected with delinquent companions.

Clark framed her hypothesis in a curious manner. A hypothesis entirely consistent with Sutherland's theory would predict that recidivist offenders (which Clark's subjects were), whether they be male or female, should be well endowed with friends at least equally committed to delinquency. True, for girls in general, differential association would predict less subcultural support than for boys, given that girls are more law-abiding than boys. But for those girls who have committed enough delinquencies to be institutionalised, it is not unlikely that they have managed to find delinquent companions to support their habitual offending. In other words, there is no reason to expect girls who have adopted a delinquent lifestyle not to have been subjected to the same criminogenic influences as boys. In fact one could well reason that, given the greater conformity of girls in general, they need a greater 'push' into delinquency, via delinquent peers, than boys. This means that differential association may be a factor in the offending of boys and girls. It can also be reasoned consistently that the explanation for the non-offending of girls and boys is the absence of subcultural support for delinquency. Girls offend less than boys because they are more conformist, and this inhibits the growth of a female delinquent subculture. Although this smacks of tautology, it is at least consistent with Sutherland's propositions.

A more ambitious study, conducted by Michael Hindelang in 1971, examined the relationship between the criminality and conformity of nearly 1000 American schoolboys and girls and the delinquent behaviour of their friends. Again, findings tended to support the theory of differential association: 'Eighty per cent of the . . . males who report having no close friends picked up by the police score low on reported delinquent involvement, while twenty six per cent of the males who report having few or more friends picked up by the police score high on reported delinquent involvement' (Hindelang, 1973:478).

Although the relationship between the delinquency of girls and their association with delinquent companions was not as strong, Hindelang's findings still lent support to the principle of differential association that 'the delinquent behaviour of one's own friends is strongly related to one's own delinquent behaviour'. Thus a large majority (73 per cent) of those girls reporting the least delinquent involvement had no delinquent friends, while only a minority (30 per cent) of girls with delinquent companions was generally law-abiding.

The attempt to trace the influence of differential association on the evolution of female crime theory is at times confounded by the failure of criminologists to make explicit their debt to Sutherland when a learning theory clearly guides their thinking. For example, Carol Smart does not list differential association among the theories of female crime she reviews, although the influence of Sutherland's work is manifest throughout *Women, Crime and Criminology*. Thus she contends that 'the realisation of a lack of access to illegitimate opportunity structures for adolescent girls and women is, of course, a most perceptive insight into an understanding of female criminality' (Smart, 1976:68).

Smart also employs a version of differential association to account for the pattern of female offending: that is, why women tend to be shoplifters rather than burglars. She claims that 'women are predominantly shoppers for household items and food and the techniques of shoplifting, unlike the techniques which might be required for other offences such as car theft or burglary, are available to them as to all shoppers' (Smart, 1976:9–10). Women who confine themselves to petty property crimes do so as a matter of their daily routine as housewives. This both normalises theft from shops and provides experience in the removal of goods from stores. In another statement, which demonstrates most clearly the influence of Sutherland's learning theory on her writing, Smart elaborates:

> The women involved in petty property offending have not required training in violence, using weapons or tools, or in specialised tasks like safe-breaking. On the contrary, the skills required can be learned in everyday experience, and socialisation in a delinquent subculture or a sophisticated criminal organisation is entirely unnecessary (Smart, 1976:15–16).

Here we see Smart employing a form of differential association to explain both the conformity of women—why they do not engage in serious, organised and violent crime—as well as why they engage in the crime they do—that is, petty, property offending.

A more recent and explicit application of differential association to the delinquency of girls comes from Peggy Giordano. Maintaining that female delinquency has recently both increased and become more versatile (her contention is borne out by the statistics), Giordano hypothesises that these changes can be traced to increased peer group support for female crime.

> It is suggested that at the very least the more delinquent, aggressive girls are receiving some kind of reference group support from other females, and possibly from other reference groups as well. This is contrasted with the traditional situation where girls may have curtailed their behaviour in part because of concern over what the other girls thought, or because their boyfriends would disapprove (Giordano, 1978:128).

Differential association explains both the previous conformity of girls—they were the recipients of an excess of definitions unfavourable to violation of the law—as well as the recent increase in female delinquency—there is now more subcultural support for delinquency in girls.

To test her predictions, Giordano administered a self-report delinquency questionnaire to a sample of institutionalised delinquent girls and to a group of high-school students. Subjects were asked how various reference groups (boys, girls and boyfriends) would react if they (the subjects) were to commit delinquencies ranging from 'picking up guys' to 'beating up on somebody'. Respondents were also required to describe their usual associates.

By confining herself to current influences, Giordano failed to examine changes over time in the peer-group support of the delinquencies of girls. As a consequence, her idea that there is now more subcultural support for criminality in girls was never tested. Nevertheless, a significant relationship was observed between the confessed delinquencies of girls and 'group affiliation'. Also challenging the common assumption that when girls do offend they are led by boys, Giordano found that although 'groups which include both males and females were particularly conducive to delinquency . . . the perception of approval from other girlfriends was significantly correlated with actual delinquency involvement' (Giordano, 1978:132). In other words, the more a girl thought that her female friends approved of crime, the more likely she was to offend. Indeed, only a small percentage of all respondents felt that trouble was most likely to occur with 'one' guy. Furthermore, over half of the delinquent sample had been members of gangs of girls.

The research considered thus far has examined the value of differential association as a predictor of crime in young females. Explicitly in response to this failure of the empirical literature to consider women, Douglas Smith (1979) conducted his ambitious survey of self-reported crimes in America. An interesting aspect of Smith's survey is that instead of asking the members of his sample to report past offending (with its usual problems of accurate recollection), they were required to predict the probability of their future (tomorrow) offending given the 'need' or 'desire'. In view of Sutherland's formulation of differential association, which includes the learning of delinquent motives, this particular wording was perhaps unfortunate. It meant that the influence of differential association on the decision to offend was left untested; subjects were already provided with a hypothetical motive and so did not need to consider this aspect of their offending.

Smith's measure of differential association was the subjects' assessment of the amount of deviance committed by their 'reference' group. They were asked 'what proportion of the people you know personally do each of the deviances [listed in the survey form] at least once a year' (Smith, 1979:188). Not surprisingly, the self-report survey revealed a greater propensity to offend among male subjects. The male:female ratio of offenders was 1.4:1. Notwithstanding the greater conformity of female subjects, delinquent subcultural support was found to be at least as good as an indicator of the likelihood of female offending as of a male offending. It accounted for 22 per cent of the variance in offending by males and 25 per cent of the variance among females. It was not, however, a sufficient explanation of the significantly greater conformity of females, as Smith demonstrated by holding constant subcultural involvement and continuing to find considerably more male than female offending. These findings make clear that although association with delinquent friends is related equally to the offending of males and females, when both sexes have the same number of delinquent friends, males still offend more than females.

Remarkably similar results were produced by Simons, Miller and Aigner (1980) who also hypothesised that the sex differential in crime was a matter of females having fewer delinquent friends. Using an even larger sample of nearly 4000 schoolboys and girls, Simons and associates administered self-report delinquency tests and also asked subjects 'to comment upon the values of their friends and upon the way their friends would be likely to react to various delinquent acts' (Simons et al., 1980:45). Differential association predicted delinquency in females as well as it predicted male offending. Moreover the greater conformity of girls revealed by the self-report questionnaire (8.8 per cent of males and 3.5 per cent of females had high delinquency scores) was found to be associated with their having fewer friends who approved of delinquency. Males were thus observed to be significantly more delinquent than females and to have more friends who favoured delinquency.

THE LEGACY OF SUTHERLAND

This review of the theoretical and empirical literature which has applied differential association to women reveals a central concern with the notion that female conformity is a function of the absence of subcultural and cultural support for female offenders. Those theorists who have attempted to test this theory empirically have met with mixed success. The early tests of the theory of differential association with girls were influenced by the conventional notion of the day that female crime was predominantly sexual in nature and that this was a function of the priority given to personal relations. In her investigations of the theory, Ruth Morris, for example, considered the 'heavy petting' of girls and the 'theft and assault' of boys. Efforts such as this to distinguish and accentuate the offending of the sexes, however, did not yield the anticipated sex differences of outlook and attitude. Morris, for one, found against her predictions that girls were not more critical than boys of delinquency in girls. Shirley Merrit Clark likewise began research assuming the delinquencies of girls to be essentially private sexual acts, removed from more general social influences and found otherwise. Boys and girls offended in comparable ways and were equally encouraged by delinquent companions.

Since these pioneering inquiries into differential association as an explanation of female crime, there has developed a more widespread appreciation of congruities in the pattern of male and female offending. Contrary to criminological predictions about the peculiarly private nature of delinquency in girls— that it is caused by an inability to form the usual socially approved set of relationships and thus manifests itself in prohibited sexual relations—research continues to highlight the significance of delinquent friends for the deviance of both sexes. Criminality, it appears, is learned in social contexts where it is regarded as an acceptable mode of behaviour. Regardless of the sex of the individual, proximity to delinquent peers conduces to lawbreaking. Notwithstanding findings such as these, criminologists have not sought to modify in any significant way Sutherland's original statement that women's experience is all a matter of their exclusion from the dominant culture, within the family, which in turn ensures their conformity. In modern formulations, the theory of differential association still entails the claim that the feminine ideal defines criminality as inappropriate for women. Women in the ideal should be passive, dependent and conventional. Women's conformity is attributed to the fact of women being taught neither the motives nor the methods of criminality because they are conventionally excluded from criminal subcultures. They are neither educated in the skills required for a life of crime nor provided the necessary training for a legitimate career. Traditional learning theory is also still found to inform modern explanations of why women engage in the few crimes that they do commit. It is suggested by writers such as Smart that women are shoplifters because this offence requires only the minimal skills of shopping, a routine function of housewives. The role of housewife, however, is said to equip women for little more than this simple crime.

What criminologists have done to women in their use of differential association is simply to assign to them fewer learning experiences and therefore fewer skills than men. The reason why women engage in such a narrow range of criminal activities is that they are seen to lack training opportunities. Although Sutherland objected to the egoism of his male subject, he acknowledged the diversity of his experiences: they might equip the male for a life of crime or conformity or both. When applied to female behaviour, learning theory strips women of access to criminogenic experiences. As a consequence, they are denied the ability to behave as interestingly as men. Women are more conformist than men because they are deemed to be not as well educated in the ways of the world. The discovery that girls who do offend are, like boys, encouraged by delinquent peers and do not appear to be transgressing for any specifically female reasons has done little to change the stereotype. Women are still thought to behave as they do because they are assigned a special domestic role which involves a sheltered and cloistered existence.

The interpretation of female behaviour in terms of the processes of exclusion of women from male learning experiences is entirely in accord with Sutherland's original theory. And yet Sutherland's influential book provides the seeds of a different and positive construction of women's conformity. In condemning the egoism of modern societies, Sutherland points approvingly to the altruism of earlier communities which ensured a more peaceable coexistence. He cites as an example of cooperative living pre-modern China where 'charity involved no stigma or disgrace whatever' (Sutherland and Cressey, 1966:101). Later in his volume, when he comes to describe the law-abiding nature of females, Sutherland fails to connect what he now calls the female attribute of 'niceness' with his earlier views on the ennobling qualities of 'charity' or 'altruism'. Thus the peaceable nature of women which Sutherland observes is drained of any positive cultural content. With the single word 'niceness', the lawfulness of women is reduced to a vapid thing. It is a matter of absence of choice (supervision) and conditioning (into anti-criminal behaviour patterns). It is stripped of any positive moral content.

The questions then to be posed about modern uses of differential association are 'why has there been no challenge to

Sutherland for this inconsistency in his conception of law-abiding behaviour?' and 'why has no-one pursued the more positive construction of conformity as altruism already hinted at by the great author?'.

4

Masculinity theory

Masculinity theory comprises two ideas: crime is symbolically masculine and masculinity supplies the motive for a good deal of crime. The qualities demanded of the criminal—daring, toughness, aggression—all exemplify maleness. The boy or man who engages in crime can demonstrate to the world that he is truly virile. As an explanation of female behaviour, masculinity theory posits the unsuitability of crime for women, thereby explaining their greater conformity. Our culture expects women to be passive, not aggressive, dependent, not audacious. The feminine woman will choose, therefore, not to engage in the symbolically male activity of law-breaking.

The masculinity theory of offending was first expounded by the American sociologist Talcott Parsons. In 1947, Parsons offered an account of the greater delinquency of boys than girls based on the structure and function of the American nuclear family (Parsons, 1954). He maintained that the principal task of women is to nurture and socialise children in the domestic sphere while men are expected to provide financial support for the entire family, performing work outside the home. All the primary public works are assigned to the male, in this functional allotment of tasks, said Parsons. The exclusive duties of the female are quite appropriately those related to the private sphere of the family. The woman devotes herself to the running of the family leaving her male partner free to get on with the business of running the public world.

This sex-based division of labour of adult family members, Parsons argued, affects boys and girls differently and accounts for the greater rebelliousness of the male. For boys, the main concern generated by the different roles performed by their parents is to divorce themselves from the feminine function (the mother's role). But this is not an easy task given the omnipresence of the mother and the absence of the father. The boy's solution is to engage in behaviour which he feels will demonstrate both his independence and difference from his mother. Accordingly he sets out to acquire a reputation for toughness and aggression. And herein lies the key to the delinquency of boys.

As the ever-present mother-figure is seen to precipitate the delinquency of boys, so she is also the reason for the greater conformity of girls. Like her brother, the female child is provided with a ready model of feminine behaviour, but in her case this poses no problem for the obvious reason that she is the same sex as her mother. The daily contact with someone performing the roles of housewife and mother is in fact beneficial. She 'has a more favourable opportunity for emotional maturing through positive identification with an adult model' (Parsons, 1954:305). The tendency of girls to be more law-abiding than boys, however, is not entirely a function of the absence of anxiety about their femininity. It is due also to the acquisition of 'feminine' attributes such as passivity and probity. These traits are encouraged by the mother who 'above all, focuses in herself the symbols of what is "good" behaviour, of conformity with the expectations of the adult respectable world' (Parsons, 1954:306).

In his assessment of the roles of men and women, Parsons does not suggest that they are symmetrical. The place of the female is distinctly inferior, in Parsons' estimation. The 'modern type of urban and industrial society', which Parsons describes, is almost fully colonised by the male. He dominates the occupational system which is 'the arena of the most important competitive process in which the individual must achieve his status'. Women, located in the family, are dependent for their position and income 'on the occupational status of one member, the husband and father'. (Parsons, 1954:303)

The ruling male culture, according to Parsons, is character-ised by rivalry. 'A man has to "win" the competition for selec-tion' for jobs 'in order to have an opportunity to prove his capacity for the higher achievements'. Parsons displays consid-erable respect for this culture of the male, in particular, the race for upward mobility through employment. 'It is in the occupational sphere,' he suggests, 'that the big things are done.' He offers his commiserations to the benighted female, precluded from this bustling and prestigious arena. He is sensi-tive to the fact that 'this drastic exclusion must serve to in-crease the inferior feelings of the woman' (Parsons, 1954:312, 313).

The female, in Parsons' scheme, is disallowed from the ultimate test of maturity and presumably consigned to a state of perpetual infancy: 'Ability to perform well and hold one's own or excel in competition is the primary realistic test of adult adequacy' (Parsons, 1955:314). But clearly this is not to be part of the female experience.

In Parson's interpretation, the fact that the female is allotted a second-rate and uninteresting function not only denies her the most demanding and satisfying experiences of the male culture. It also assigns her to an inferior caste whose charac-teristics are despised and repudiated by the dominant group. Women, maintains Parsons, exist to foster in their children a sense of ethical behaviour which will fit them for society. But women are not appreciated for this work they are required to perform. On the contrary, the femaleness of the function of socialising the next generation into the 'expectations of the adult world' has the extraordinary effect of casting doubt on the very value of 'being good'. The boy observes the virtues of the mother, but also perceives her lowly status and so seeks to divorce himself from all that she represents—hence 'the strong tendency for boyish behaviour to run in antisocial . . . direc-tions' (Parsons, 1954:306). To Parsons, this seems a perfectly sensible thing for the boy to do in view of Parsons' estimation of the respective worth of the male and the female culture.

Parsons expresses concern about the damage wrought by the association of 'good' actions with the quality of being female. The ill effects of this conjunction, he says, are not confined to the precipitation of delinquency in boys but extend to the entire adult sphere. Indeed Parsons goes so far as to suggest that this unfortunate association permeates the entire Western approach to virtue: 'much of our Western ambivalence toward ethical values has its roots in this tradition' (Parsons, 1954:306).

It is not difficult to detect where Parsons' sympathies lie in his account of the 'good' mother and the 'bad' boy. He describes delinquency in the youthful male as 'boyish behaviour' and suspects that mothers secretly, though 'usually unconsciously', admire the endeavours of their sons to dissociate themselves from their mothers. He notes that the bad boy may have 'winning qualities in other respects' and even attract greater approbation than his less adventurous brother. 'She [the mother] may quite frequently treat such a "bad" son as her favorite as compared with a "sissy" brother who conforms with all her overt expectations much better' (Parsons, 1954:306).

The mother's illicit admiration of the naughty boy who strives to prove his masculinity in anti-social ways is reflected in the wider culture. Parsons maintains the existence of a cult of 'compulsive masculinity' in Western society. The Western man is 'peculiarly susceptible to the appeal of an adolescent type of assertively masculine behaviour and attitude' (Parsons, 1954:309). As a consequence, the Western way of life is typified not only by its competitive aspect but also by its aggression. Parsons even refers to an 'idealisation' of aggressive masculinity in Western men who are egged on by females who also have been taught to find this attribute appealing.

Modern industrial society, to Parsons, is indisputably male in character. It is distinctive in the value it accords competition, achievement and aggression. The very quality of masculinity impresses. The quality of femininity is low in prestige. Any behaviour associated with the male is considered to be attractive, even those forms which society ostensibly condemns as positively bad. Any behaviour associated with the female is regarded as unappealing, even if society professes to praise it as a positive good.

Parsons has no quarrel with the alleged perceptions of the adolescent boy who 'soon discovers that in certain vital respects women are considered inferior to men, that it would hence be shameful for him to grow up to be like a woman' (Parsons, 1954:305). One imagines Parsons' considerable relief that he is able to make his observations about the nature of his society, in particular its overt and covert masculinity, from the secure and exalted position of the male.

In 1951, another American sociologist, George Grosser, adopted Parsons' analysis of gender roles and applied it directly to the offending of boys and girls. Both male and female delinquency, argued Grosser, are expressions of gender role. As prospective breadwinners, boys are principally concerned with power, prestige and money. As future wives and mothers, girls are preoccupied with relationships rather than material accumulation or self-aggrandisement. It follows that when a boy commits a delinquent act such as stealing, he is expressing his concern with material gain. When a girl engages in delinquent behaviour, she, too, is expressing an interest (in boys) which is appropriate to her gender role. As a consequence, girls are less likely to steal than to engage in sexual promiscuity, while those girls who do steal are, nevertheless, engaging in 'role-supportive' behaviour. For example, they steal items which will make them more attractive to the opposite sex.

Acknowledging a debt to both Parsons and Grosser, Cohen strongly endorsed the idea that delinquency expresses gender when he published *Delinquent Boys* (1955). Although the principal theme developed by Cohen is the effect of thwarted aspirations on working-class youth, he also expended some effort on advancing the thesis that crime verifies masculinity, with its necessary corollary that it is, in the main, an unsuitable activity for girls. Cohen also addressed the issue of female offending. Believing, like Grosser, that girls are essentially law-abiding, Cohen developed Parsons' idea that girls effectively socialise into conformity. He contended that girls positively avoid violent forms of delinquency which have masculine connotations.

The delinquency in which girls do engage, which Cohen maintained is essentially sexual in nature, is also explicable in terms of their training for womanhood. The social fact that girls are destined to become wives and mothers ensures their preoccupation with the task of finding a mate. To achieve this goal they must make themselves attractive and cultivate their social and sexual skills. Cohen argued that 'sexual delinquency is one kind of meaningful response to the most characteristic, most central and most ego-involved problem of the female role: the establishment of satisfactory relationships with the opposite sex' (Cohen, 1955:147). Cohen also thought that girls were actively socialised to behave in passive and conformist ways.

MODERN MASCULINITY THEORY

In contemporary criminology, there has been a remarkably high degree of fidelity to Parsons' original conception of sex roles among both feminist and more traditional writers. In 1969 the Canadian criminologist, Marie Andrée Bertrand, offered a version of masculinity theory, suggesting that

> While our culture condones and even expects a certain amount of acting out and aggressive behaviour in young boys, it is less tolerant of the foibles of young girls. Physical strength, shrewdness in business matters, for instance, are very compatible with our 'ideal typus' of the 'normal' adult male, while such attributes—oftentimes necessary for the performance of recurrent crimes—are not usually associated with femininity because society does not want women trained or practised in such matters (Bertrand, 1969:74).

Similarly, in 1973 Dale Hoffman Bustamante observed that the different socialisation of the sexes encouraged girls to be more obedient and law-abiding: 'Females have been taught to conform to more rigid standards and rewarded for such behaviour, whereas males are told to conform, yet rewarded for flouting many conventional standards' (Hoffman Bustamante, 1973:120).

While Bertrand and Hoffman Bustamante offered accounts of female behaviour which were explicit in their reliance on the idea of an acquired male and female character, later theories of female crime informed by a feminist perspective drew more indirectly on the idea of the passive female. For example, in 1976 Dorie Klein and June Kress provided an explanation of the pettiness of female crime in terms of women's social disadvantages rather than their individual proclivities: 'Women's lack of participation in "big time" crime highlights the larger class structure of sexism that is reproduced in the illegal marketplace' (Klein and Kress, 1976:41).

The influence of masculinity theory's model of woman on these authors becomes apparent only upon scrutiny of their explanation of crimes committed by women which do not accord with their oppressed social position. Klein and Kress slip into a form of psychologism, curiously at odds with their structural approach, when they encounter women behaving in ways which seem to challenge their traditional role. While female shoplifting is interpreted as a logical outcome of the social position of women as housewives in 'straight' society, the less conventional female robber is deemed to be a mere product of her conditioning: she is typically an accomplice who thereby maintains her gender-prescribed passivity. And again, the woman who flouts convention by engaging in prostitution is not observed to be committing an economic crime; she is performing 'the same functions of sexual work and nurturance that other women do'.

All this is not intended to detract from the pioneering endeavour of Klein and Kress to provide an analysis of 'sexism . . . in the illegal marketplace' in terms of the oppression of women as a class. The identification of lapses in their theorising—when their ideas appear to owe more to the thinking of Grosser and Cohen than to any sort of class or stratification theory—is a manifestation of the vigour of masculinity theory rather than an indictment of this attempt to develop a feminist criminology.

Sometimes the genealogy of ideas in the evolution of these criminological theories is obscure or understated, or merely implicit. In the work of Carol Smart, the influential feminist criminologist, one can find lines of argument which have kinship with Cohen's theory, but the connections are never fully articulated. The value of tracing these connections lies in the fact that *Women, Crime and Criminology* remains the most intellectually rigorous and theoretically sophisticated work in the field.[1] With such a prominent role in the literature, it is vital to distinguish those parts of Smart's thinking which are reminiscent of traditional accounts of the passive female from those more explicitly informed by contemporary critiques of women's social role.

Like Klein and Kress, Smart maintains a focus on the structural inequalities of women's position when she considers those crimes which bear an obvious relation to women's traditional social functions. Her account of women's shoplifting, for example, is in terms of their historically determined material circumstances. Smart observes that 'in industrial societies like the United Kingdom and the United States of America . . . [W]omen are predominantly shoppers for household items and food and the techniques of shoplifting, unlike the techniques which might be required for other offences, such as car theft and burglary, are as available to them as to all shoppers' (Smart, 1976:9–10).

It is when Smart seeks to explain women's involvement in what at first sight would appear to be unfeminine crimes that signs of traditional masculinity theory appear. Thus the exceptional woman who engages in the crime of receiving stolen goods becomes a victim of the model of the inert female. She is a passive associate who does not participate in the original theft or burglary. According to Smart,

> This 'passivity' is in keeping with the woman's role especially where stolen goods are hidden or used in the home. Furthermore it is frequently the case that women will conceal stolen goods for those with whom they have some kind of personal relationship, for example husbands, lovers or sons, and they therefore become implicated in criminal behaviour through 'family loyalty' (Smart, 1976:15).

The economic crime of receipt of stolen goods thus is transformed into a mere vehicle for expressing traditionally feminine traits of affection, loyalty and passivity.

TESTING THE THEORY

Notwithstanding the considerable influence exerted by masculinity theory in the literature on women and crime, there have been surprisingly few attempts to verify the hypothesis. Considering first that strand of the theory which maintains that the delinquency of boys is a reaction to the threat of becoming feminised by overexposure to an adult female, the investigations of Silverman and Dinitz (1974) provide some empirical support.

Employing a sample of institutionalised delinquent boys they examined the relationship between, among other things, 'compulsive masculinity' and matriarchal homes using their own measure of this trait. The test instrument was designed to determine 'the boys' self-identification with tough behaviour' as well as 'sexual athleticism' (Silverman and Dinitz, 1974:505). It included such items as weapon-carrying, drinking, kicking a fallen opponent and maintaining a reputation as a tough guy. Subjects were also asked to assess their own masculinity as were the supervisors from the home from which the boys were drawn. Finally, subjects were tested for their impulsiveness, hostility and their predisposition to engage in excitement-oriented, high-risk activities.

Consistent with that part of Parsons' theory which suggests that boys who are deprived of male role models become compulsively masculine, Silverman and Dinitz found that 'delinquent boys from female-based households were more hyper-masculine than delinquents from other types of households' (Silverman and Dinitz, 1974:511). These boys were also observed to be more impulsive, more hostile, and more prone to engage in exciting, high-risk activities. Thus a correlation was discovered between compulsive masculinity and anti-social tendencies.

The impact of masculinity theory on the criminology of women was not felt in the empirical literature until 1979 when the results of three investigations were reported. Although all three studies were conducted in America, a different test of 'masculinity' was used by each investigator.

Students attending a midwestern university (99 men and 83 women) were surveyed by Cullen, Golden and Cullen (1979) in their research into the relationship between self-reported delinquency and masculinity. Subjects were asked about their involvement in violent, property, drug and status offences and then tested for 'self-perceived male-behavioural traits' which comprised a selection from the attributes identified by Rosenkrantz (1968) as 'stereotypically masculine traits'. These were aggression, independence, objectivity, dominance, competitiveness and self-confidence in relation to which subjects were asked to rate themselves on 'a four-point scale ranging from "not at all" to "a large extent"'.

Although findings were in the direction predicted by the theory, the possession of masculine traits was not a complete explanation of the greater amount of offending admitted to by male subjects. Notwithstanding the fact that 'male' traits significantly and positively predicted delinquency in all but the drug category, when the factor of masculinity was held constant, males still committed more delinquencies. That is to say, 'masculine' males reported more delinquency than 'masculine' females. Thus the greater delinquency of male subjects was not fully explained by the possession of masculine traits. The authors tentatively concluded that 'in general, our data lend some support to the masculinity hypotheses' (Cullen, et al., 1979:308).

Instead of confining herself to a simple measure of masculinity, the American criminologist Cathy Spatz Widom (1979) made use of both masculine and feminine traits (employing the Bem Sex-Role Inventory) as well as adjectives indicating social desirability in her research into the effects of masculinity and femininity on delinquency. Her subjects comprised 73 women in custody awaiting trial and a control group of twenty non-offending women who were roughly matched for socioeconomic status, race and education. According to their responses, subjects were sorted into four personality types: 'androgynous' or high masculinity and high femininity; 'masculine' or high masculinity and low femininity; 'feminine' or high femininity and low masculinity; and 'undifferentiated' or low masculinity and low femininity.

Widom's findings were mixed. Although the offender group was observed to be no more 'masculine' than the non-offending women, within the sample of criminal women, 'femininity' was found to be inversely related to criminal involvement. The less feminine the offender, the greater the number of kinds of previous convictions. In other words, low femininity was a better predictor of recidivism (employed as a measure of criminality) than high masculinity. Widom determined that 'the existing data . . . are not persuasive that . . . high levels of masculinity are major factors in female criminality' (Widom, 1979:376–7).

The third test of masculinity theory reported in 1979 was conducted by Neal Shover, Stephen Norland, Jennifer James and William Thornton. In terms of the number of subjects (over 1000) this is by far the most ambitious piece of research into masculinity theory undertaken. It is therefore unfortunate that it made use of what are probably the crudest measures of masculinity and femininity of those considered here.

Shover and colleagues drew their sample from male and female students attending eighteen schools in Nashville who were administered a self-report delinquency test. Among other things, subjects were required to respond to two scales designed to test their masculinity and femininity. In view of the small number of items comprising each scale it is worthwhile listing them in full. The 'Traditional Masculinity Expectations Scale' consisted of the following five items:

1   I expect to pay for activities when on a date.
2   I expect to fix things like the car.
3   If I marry, I would expect to provide most of the income for my family.
4   I expect to ask someone for a date rather than being asked.
5   If I marry, I would expect to take responsibility for major family decisions, such as buying a home or a car.

The 'Traditional Femininity Expectations Scale' comprised these items:

1   If I marry, I would expect to be mainly responsible for housework, whether outside the home or not.
2   Before going out at night, I expect to tell my parents where I am going.
3   I expect to help take care of younger children in the family or neighbourhood.
4   I expect to get married and raise a family rather than get a job in the business world.
5   If I marry, I would expect to move to another city if my spouse changed jobs.

The results of this investigation were reported in several articles published by various combinations of the researchers and several other colleagues. Each of these papers has considered slightly different aspects of the survey.

In their discussion of the survey, Thornton and James (1979) considered only the masculinity scale together with subjects' comments on how strongly they felt each expectation was held for their own behaviour by parents and friends. Replicating the results of other self-report studies, they found that 'the greatest percentage of girls are involved in a comparatively low amount of delinquency, while the largest proportion of boys is highly delinquent' (Thornton and James, 1979:231).

Those girls who were delinquent, however, were not, as expected, observed to be more masculine than law-abiding girls. For boys, the relationship between masculinity and delinquency depended on the nature of their belief about how others saw them. Although boys who evinced masculine expectations were not more delinquent than those with lower scores on this scale, those males who believed that others held comparatively weak masculine expectations of them were found to be highly involved in delinquency.

The implications of these findings for masculinity theory are, as Thornton and James note, mixed. Although they fail to lend support to the thesis that the possession of masculine expectations predicts delinquency in boys and girls, they are consistent with Parsons' idea of 'reaction formation': that anti-social behaviour is a solution to a boy's anxiety about others perceiving him as unmasculine. This is of course unhelpful for an explanation of female crime.

In 1979 all four authors of this investigation also presented an interpretation of their findings (Shover et al., 1979). Here the effects of both masculinity and femininity scales were considered. In addition, self-reported delinquencies were divided into aggressive and property offences. Again the inquiry disclosed that for both boys and girls, masculine expectations were unrelated to delinquency, regardless of whether it was aggressive or property-offending. That is, subjects with masculine self-expectations were not significantly more involved in aggressive or property crime than those with low masculinity scores. Relationships between femininity scores were not as straightforward. Consistent with masculinity theory's prediction, there was an inverse relationship between girls' feminine expectations and aggressive delinquency. Girls with strong feminine expectations were less involved in aggressive delinquencies than were those with low scores on this scale. This was the only statistically significant relationship observed, however, between the two gender personality scales and the two types of delinquencies for both sexes. Summarising the implications of their findings, Shover and colleagues concluded that 'taken as a whole there is only limited support for masculinity theory' (Shover et al., 1979:169).

More recently still, Pamela Loy and Stephen Norland (1981) put the results of this investigation to further use. This time subjects' responses to the masculinity and femininity scales were reclassified into four groups. Like Widom, who used the 'Bem Inventory', Loy and Norland designated answers as 'androgynous' (high masculinity and high femininity), 'traditionally feminine' (high femininity and low masculinity), traditionally masculine (high masculinity and low femininity), and 'undifferentiated' (low masculinity and low femininity). Self-reported delinquencies were also regrouped into status offences as well as property and aggressive offences.

Instead of predicting a direct and positive relationship between masculine expectations and delinquency and an inverse relationship between feminine expectations and delinquency, the authors predicted that the offending of androgynous and undifferentiated males and females would be more similar in frequency than that of traditional males and females. Framing the hypothesis in this way, the inquiry now produced significant relationships between gender role expectations and offending. As anticipated, androgynous males and females were more similar in the frequency of each type of delinquency than traditional females and males. Also as expected, less differentiated females and males displayed more similar patterns of delinquency than their traditional counterparts. A further finding which Loy and Norland considered noteworthy was that 'undifferentiated females report more involvement in some forms of delinquency than undifferentiated males. For property and aggressive offenses, the delinquency scores for females exceeded those reported by males' (Loy and Norland, 1981:279). Moreover, intra-sex comparison revealed that undifferentiated females had the highest level of involvement in all delinquencies while the reverse was true for males.

After the elimination of 'masculine' females (there were too few cases) the researchers theorised that masculinity theory should predict that androgynous females (the next 'most masculine' group) would report the highest level of involvement in delinquency because they held the most traditionally male expectations of the remaining groups tested. But this was not the case. In fact androgynous females reported the lowest level of involvement in two of the offence groups, a finding which strikes at the foundation of the theory. As a consequence the authors were forced to concede that 'something other than simply masculinization is operating to produce these within-sex patterns. The issue of why undifferentiated females tend to be more involved in delinquency compared to other females while undifferentiated males report relatively fewer incidents of delinquency compared to other males remains' (Loy and Norland, 1981:279).

These unanswered questions in the findings of Loy and Norland are worrying enough, but even more disturbing is a further fundamental flaw in the inquiry relating to the key analytic concepts. Although sorting subjects' responses into 'androgynous', 'undifferentiated' and so on does manage to produce significant relationships between delinquency and masculinity where earlier categorisation of these data failed, it is by no means clear what these findings reveal about the nature of juvenile delinquents and juvenile crime. As Loy and Norland candidly explain (1981:283), these concepts 'lack an informative theoretical meaning. They represent nominal categories whose theoretical meaning is at best vague'.

A basis for further concern is the test instrument which the authors of this inquiry suggest is a substantial improvement on all previous measures of masculinity. Loy and Norland are highly critical of other attempts to test the masculinity hypothesis. For example, Cullen and his colleagues are said to employ a measure of gender which is 'bi-polar and unidimensional' (recall that Cullen's subjects rated themselves according to six masculinity traits). Moreover the 'Bem Inventory' (which was used by Widom although her investigation is not mentioned here) is regarded as defective because it treats gender 'solely as self-judged personality attributes'. But does the instrument used by Loy and Norland represent any real improvement?

Although they are dissatisfied with the concepts of masculinity employed by their predecessors, Loy and Norland offer no cogent reasons why their own test is any better. Their claim that their measure alone 'reflects variations in feminine and masculine role expectations', rather than simply 'defining convergence as masculinization of females' ignores the fact that the Bem Inventory also has masculinity and femininity scales and, as Widom demonstrated, allows results to be analysed in terms of 'androgyny' and 'undifferentiated sex'. Moreover the Loy and Norland test is actually less calibrated than Bem in that it reduces gender differences to ten as opposed to 40 characteristics. Indeed, its ability to be used in a fourfold analysis in terms of 'androgyny' and so on should not obscure the fact that it relies on simple stereotypes of the sexes. Although Loy and Norland conduct some comparatively sophisticated statistical analyses of their findings, these analytical insights are necessarily limited by their reliance on a handful of social 'expectations' which are thought to represent the quintessence of masculinity and femininity. While condemning others for polarising the sexes and adhering to unidimensional concepts of masculinity and femininity, the view of masculinity to which the authors subscribe focuses exclusively on initiating and paying for dates, fixing cars and anticipating the role of a breadwinner who makes decisions for the family. And the core of femininity is apparently to be found in a girl's expectation that she will grow up to be a housewife (rather than a breadwinner), who is willing to change city if her husband changes job and who displays an interest in children.

Now it is perfectly conceivable that an assertive, independent girl, one whom the Bem Inventory would characterise as high on masculinity, would appear to be a traditional female on the Loy and Norland scale simply because of a realistic appraisal of the limited occupational opportunities for women and the enforced dependence which comes with having to assume total responsibility for children. In fact, it is highly probable that the Loy and Norland test taps something in its respondents quite different from the Bem test and there is no obvious reason why the trait it measures is closer to the essence of femininity (whatever that might be) than Bem or any other test of gender-related personality. The origin of the items comprising the Loy and Norland test does not guarantee its superiority at measuring masculinity and femininity. The provenance of the two sets of social expectations it employs to typify the sexes was a 'pre-test' sample of adolescents who were asked to select behaviour they thought to be masculine and feminine. However the authors do not explain why this mode of constructing a test instrument should produce a more reliable measure of personality differences between the sexes than any standard measure developed by psychologists.

An endeavour to bring together the empirical literature for the purposes of verification of masculinity theory is to a large extent confounded by the many different empirical methods employed by criminologists. For one thing, the type of subjects interviewed in each inquiry varied considerably. Whereas Silverman and Dinitz used an all-male sample of institutionalised delinquents with no controls, Widom employed an all-female sample of women in prison and a small control group. While the Cullen and Shover studies both administered tests to male and to female subjects, the former inquiry considered the self-reported delinquencies of adults (university students) while the latter relied on interviews with schoolchildren. The disconnected nature of the research discussed in this chapter is also apparent from the range of measures of masculinity employed. Silverman and Dinitz, and Cullen and his associates only considered masculinity traits. The investigations of Widom and of Shover and colleagues examined both masculinity and femininity. No two studies used the same test.

In view of the lack of collaboration between researchers into masculinity theory, it is perhaps not surprising that an attempt to synthesise the evidence is unable to yield an unambiguous result. The observations of Silverman and Dinitz and those of Thornton and James go some way to supporting

Parsons' theory of reaction formation: that boys who believe that others perceive them as unmasculine compensate by engaging in delinquent acts. Indeed masculinity theory seems to have had its greatest empirical success in establishing correlations between compulsive or hyper-masculinity and delinquency. Where researches have focused on more conventional modes of masculinity, findings have been more equivocal.

Although their study was not a complete explanation of the greater conformity of girls, Cullen and colleagues did find support for the theory that masculine traits predict delinquency. The findings of Widom and of Shover and associates, however, ran in the opposite direction. Their inquiries revealed that masculine traits were unrelated to delinquency, although less feminine (as opposed to more masculine) women were more delinquent than their more feminine counterparts. Put differently, that research which made use of a femininity index found this scale, rather than the masculinity index, predicted delinquency for females but in a negative direction. While females who exhibit male traits are not likely to be more delinquent than those who do not, those who fail to display feminine traits are more prone to delinquency. Empirical testing of masculinity theory so far has failed therefore in its endeavour to explain the greater known delinquency of males.

THE STRENGTH OF PARSONS' STEREOTYPE

The use of a variety of concepts and measures of masculinity (and of femininity) to test masculinity theory does not reflect simply the personal preferences of social scientists working in the field. There is a problem which runs much deeper. It is the problem of a powerful stereotype of women in criminology which is based almost exclusively on a deep conviction about the different and unequal natures of the sexes, not on empirical proof. That stereotype of woman was nurtured in sociology by Talcott Parsons, imported into criminology by Cohen, and has maintained its privileged status within the discipline with little critical comment.

The continued prominence of the idea that a narrow set of traits connected with femininity dictates the criminality and the conformity of women is perhaps surprising in view of researchers' failure to reach any agreement about the precise natures of the sexes. Criminologists have persisted with their claims that a constrained female character associated with a constrained domestic role determines the constraint of women as law-breakers despite considerable confusion about each of these variables. As Ann Constantinople explains the state of the art, the nature of masculinity and femininity have yet to be clearly explicated: 'We are dealing with an abstract concept that seems to summarize some dimension of reality important for many people, but we are hard pressed as scientists to come up with any clear definition of the concept or indeed any unexceptionable criteria for its measurement' (Constantinople, 1973:390).

The dilemma for the criminologist in adopting such terms as masculinity and femininity with a view to predicting criminality scientifically is that 'both theoretically and empirically they seem to be among the muddiest concepts in the psychologist's vocabulary'. They are slippery concepts because, at first glance, common sense would seem to dictate that they must be related to criminality, while on closer scrutiny, the relationship is less clear. Those who theorise the significance of masculinity for criminality (and femininity for conformity) have never managed to specify exactly what it is about masculinity and femininity which triggers this behaviour, let alone define these concepts in a consistent and convincing manner. Nor have they endeavoured to establish empirically that there are such things as 'masculinity' and 'femininity', before setting out their theories. As Box observes (1983:175) in his critique of the school, 'many writers . . . assume that the independent variables—the sex role stereotypes of "aggressiveness" and "competition" for males, and "passivity" and "dependence" for females—are so well known that no documentation is needed'.

As we saw in tracing the idea from Parsons to Smart, the assumed connection between masculinity, femininity and crime has failed to develop beyond a vague notion that women are socialised in a manner which equips them poorly for offending. The adoption of masculinity theory by feminists has not yielded the sort of critical interpretation of women's role and character that one might have expected from those who profess a more discriminating approach to the study of sex differences. It is therefore not surprising that those who have sought to test these ideas empirically have been confounded by conceptual imprecision; that they can agree about neither the appropriate tests of masculinity and femininity nor the type of subjects to administer them to, nor even the sort of behaviour for which to test them. Is it frequency of all criminal behaviour which relates to masculinity, or does masculinity only explain particular delinquencies? To clarify, if 'aggressiveness' is the aspect of masculinity which criminologists maintain leads to delinquency (and recall that Albert Cohen argued that a tough, rebellious image is what boys equate with masculinity and that the desire for such an image is what precipitates criminality), it seems foolish to argue that all types of criminal behaviour are thus motivated when one considers the variety of activities outlawed. The Australian criminologist, Jocelynne Scutt, illustrates this point when she asks:

> Could it be said that every act of murder is 'aggressive'? Or that murder 'with a blunt instrument' is aggressive, murder by painless poisoning 'passive' or 'non aggressive'? Is writing a false cheque passive? aggressive? Is persuading an American to buy the Tower Bridge, or a Londoner to buy the Brooklyn Bridge, or either to buy the Sydney Harbour Bridge, aggressive? Shoplifting aggressive? passive? (Scutt, 1978a:6).

A further quandry for the criminologist interested in testing masculinity theory empirically concerns the failure of social scientists until now to relate a clearly articulated theory of masculinity and femininity to a measure of these concepts. As we have seen, Loy and Norland are refreshingly candid about the 'theoretical meaning' of their concepts of gender-related personality types as being 'at best vague'. The problem is that while a certain score on a so-called 'masculinity index' might predict consistently a certain amount of delinquency in the respondent, this cannot provide conclusive proof of the hypothesis. The reason is this: although it is clear that something is being measured by the test, and that there is a correlation between that element and delinquency, it is by no means clear that that thing is masculinity, nor that the relationship between the indicator of delinquency and the delinquency itself is a causal one. Certainly none of the attempts to prove the hypothesis so far have sought to ascertain whether the subjective meaning of a particular delinquent act was related to some aspect of masculinity or femininity by actually putting the question to delinquent subjects.

The conceptual and empirical difficulties confronting masculinity theory are easy to establish. There is no clear and uncontroversial definition of the female persona and there are no uncontested findings indicating a positive correlation between that character and women's greater conformity. And yet criminologists are still theorising confidently in the language of Parsons so that there persists a depiction of women in ways inimical to their interests. Criminologists continue to assume that crime for females is a form of expression of gender role. It is associated with legitimate female endeavours to find a mate or sustain a relationship with a male; violent or aggressive crime is avoided because it is inconsistent with the feminine ideal.

Criminologists, through their insistence on so narrowly defining the gender-appropriate attitudes and behaviour of the female, leave women little room to act with initiative, assertiveness or intelligence. The female stereotype of Parsons in the forties and of Cohen in the fifties has undergone few changes in the hands of criminologists of a more feminist persuasion. Parsons saw women as passively 'good'. Cohen depicted the female as 'sociable and timid, but inactive, unambitious and uncreative' (Child in Cohen, 1955:143). The images of women employed by latter-day exponents of masculinity theory are in the same mould. Although these modern theorists speak in terms of the pernicious effects of the gender roles imposed on women, rather than regarding them as appropriate and functional, they advance nevertheless a view of women as at least as controlled, as conformist and as ineffectual as Parsons conceived.

In their wholesale acceptance of gender socialisation, contemporary criminologists continue to expunge the agency of women. Their conviction that socialisation is a thoroughgoing process does not admit of an alternative view of the facts, that women may be critical of the gender messages they receive, that they may actively oppose instructions to be passive and to comply. Criminologists have failed to canvass the possibility that women may both accommodate and resist admonitions to adopt traditionally feminine characteristics and values.

Feminist writers in other disciplines are increasingly coming to the view that women are not simply the products of successful social training. American education writer Jean Anyon, for example, concedes that 'most women learn what is socially approved and often behave in ways that are expected'. But socialisation, she maintains, is rarely complete. Few women accept or reject fully the full range of 'sex-role appropriate attitudes and behaviours' (Anyon, 1983:19). Arthur Brittan and Mary Maynard (1984:72), who have examined the learned nature of sexism and racism, argue in a similar fashion that 'the reality of the socialization process' refutes the notion of woman as a *tabula rasa*. 'On the contrary, everywhere there is opposition, resistance, and counter-socialization.' Feminists writing about criminology have yet to consider the implications of these arguments. This chapter demonstrates that they still accept uncritically the proposition that women are thoroughly oppressed and subjugated by a sexist society.

5

Conformity as control

With their focus on the impetus to offend, most criminologists are mistaken about the central question of their discipline, according to Travis Hirschi (1969). Criminality does not need explaining. It is unnecessary to look for the 'push' to commit a crime because human beings are by nature immoral; they will engage in both social and anti-social activities unless something intervenes. The task of the criminologist therefore is to explain the motives of the law-abiding.

In setting up this challenge to the orthodox approach to crime, Hirschi undertook to provide the building blocks of a new theory of conformity which has come to be known as the 'control' school. Hirschi's key idea is that society has developed a variety of ways of 'controlling' its members and inhibiting their natural tendency to deviate. These social forms of control fall into four broad categories: attachment, commitment, involvement and belief. To the extent that a person is attached to conventional people, is committed to and involved in conventional institutions and behaviour (through, say, work and leisure activities), and believes in the rules of conventional society, that person will choose not to offend. The essence of the theory is succinctly explained by a latter-day exponent of Hirschi's ideas, Steven Box:

> Occurrence of special circumstances is not necessary to bring about freedom to deviate; freedom is there all the time as a human possibility. It is lost when human beings surrender them-

selves to others' reputations and moralities. It is regained, perhaps only momentarily, when they cease to care about others or their own social selves, or find segments of conventional morality distasteful (Box, 1981:132).

Although the term 'anomie' has come to be associated with Robert Merton and strain theory in criminological circles, in the sense in which Durkheim originally conceived it, it is of more intrinsic importance to control theory than to any modern conception of strain. Indeed, in *Causes of Delinquency*, Hirschi prefaces his exposition of his theory with an excerpt from Durkheim's *Suicide* (1952:209): 'The more weakened the groups to which [the individual] belongs, the less he depends on them, the more he consequently depends only on himself and recognizes no other rules of conduct than what are founded on his private interests.'

To verify his theory, Hirschi administered self-report delinquency tests to 1300 American metropolitan schoolboys in 1964 together with questions designed to measure their attachment to parents (for example, does your parent know where you are when you're out and who you're with?), to their school (assessed by school performance and liking for school), to delinquent and non-delinquent peers, as well as their commitment to, and involvement in, conventional actions (like homework) and respect for the law (in particular, the police).

Results were generally as predicted. Thus 'the intimacy of communication between child and parent' was strongly and inversely related to delinquency. Good school records and liking school predicted low delinquent involvement. Boys with delinquent friends were significantly more delinquent that those with law-abiding friends, while boys with high conventional aspirations tended to be non-delinquent, as did those who 'respected the law'.

For the criminologist interested in the discipline's conception of women, there are several notable features about Hirschi's work. One concerns Hirschi's endeavour to set himself apart from his colleagues who asked the standard criminological question 'Why do people offend?' and who then, with some logic, proceeded to study males—the bulk of the offender population. Hirschi proclaims his difference in posing the opposite question 'Why don't people offend?' but then, in the same manner as his colleagues whom he seeks to repudiate, selects a male population to investigate. This overlooks the fact that it would make more sense to concentrate on females as the substantially more law-abiding sex. Hirschi therefore does not pursue the logic of his own argument that criminologists should reorient their thinking by making conformity, rather than criminality, the central object of study. Instead, he maintains the usual focus on the male.

Why does Hirschi study males when he is interested in conformity? A possible explanation is the power of the criminological convention of investigating the male. However central or extraneous is the male to the theoretical construct, the male remains the apparently obvious point of concern. In Hirschi's case, the decision to consider male rather than female behaviour may simply reflect an intellectual tradition of making criminology the study of the male.

The possibility that we are talking about an unconscious but entrenched preference among criminologists for explicating male rather than female activity is strengthened by the discovery that Hirschi began his project with an ample sample of both male and female subjects. Indeed Hirschi explains, in some detail, his empirical method for eliminating bias from his samples by referring to both male and female cases. Then, unaccountably and without comment, he discards his female respondents and the research project becomes a study of social control as it applies to the male. From this one can infer that professional criminologists regard it as perfectly right not to cater for the female experience in the tests of their theory, even when that theory is presented as non-sex-specific.

A second indication that Hirschi is not even-handed in his treatment of the sexes comes from his portrayal of the law-abiding male. This person poses a striking contrast to prior characterisations of the conforming female. Hirschi's conventional male possesses an admirable set of positive and instrumental attributes. Earlier depictions of the law-abiding person as female are virtually antithetical to Hirschi's male model. Hirschi performs an almost undetectable sleight of hand in transforming criminology's conception of conventionality. As the law-abiding subject assumes a male status, his chief attributes become ennobling rather than incapacitating.

To comprehend fully the extent of the transformation wrought by Hirschi, we must juxtapose Hirschi's conforming male with the orthodox view of the conforming female. According to Hirschi, the qualities of the law-abiding person are all consistent with the role of the responsible, hard-working individual engrossed in vocational work. Obedience to the law entails a sensible and rational calculation not to place at risk the gains of a career by being found criminal. We know that Hirschi is talking here about men and not women (though he fails so to qualify his theory) because he describes the male role and the male concerns of breadwinner. This conforming male of Hirschi's is an admirable character; he is an energetic, intelligent and rational being. If we now consider statements about the law-abiding person made by Hirschi's predecessors, who associated conformity with femininity, one finds the very same behaviour interpreted in a wholly negative fashion. Cohen, Sutherland and Parsons, when they conceived the conforming person to be female, found her to be passive, dependent and generally lacking any critical faculties. It was the criminal male, in these accounts, who possessed the instrumental virtues. As Hirschi changes the field of study, from the criminal man to the conforming man, so the enriching qualities of masculinity now attach to conventionality and it is delinquency which is devalued as a symptom of emotional immaturity. Hirschi therefore alters our vision of conformity as he conceives of the conforming person as male, not female.

What all this seems to indicate is a profound criminological tendency to devalue the female and value the male even when they are doing precisely the same things. Hirschi's law-abiding male is actively sensitive to the opinions of others. The conforming female, according to Cohen, is inertly dependent. Hirschi's male cares about the wishes and expectations of others. Criminology's female is a slave to social approval. Hirschi's male invests 'time, energy, himself in a certain line of activity—say, getting an education, building up a business, acquiring a reputation for virtue' (Hirschi, 1969:20). He decides to remain law-abiding because this is an intelligent response to his positive commitments to, and involvement in, conventional society. The law-abiding female, in strain and masculinity theory, is passive: she lacks invention and initiative.

Hirschi's conforming male is 'engrossed in conventional activities'. He is 'too busy doing conventional things to find time to engage in deviant behaviour'. He is 'tied to appointments, deadlines, working hours, plans and the like, so the opportunity to commit deviant acts rarely arises' (Hirschi, 1969:22). Criminology's conforming female is distinguished by her inactivity and lack of achievement. In her feminine role, the conventional female is in a state of being (attractive), not doing, and her conformity is a clear expression of this passivity.

The tenacity of the criminological tendency to find positive value in male activity, whether it entails lawful or criminal enterprises, is thrown into even sharper relief by the work of Hagan, Simpson and Gillis (1979). This inquiry represents one of the most extensively theorised pieces of research which has sought to apply Hirschi's control theory to the female. A key hypothesis of the investigation was that females experience more informal (familial) controls than boys, who are more subject to official (legal) controls than girls. Hagan interviewed over 600 Canadian high-school students about the extent to which their parents knew of their whereabouts when they were away from home as a test of informal control, a test also employed by Hirschi. Hagan also asked subjects about their contact with the police (formal control) and their undetected offending. As predicted, when delinquency was held constant, boys had experienced more contact with police while girls were more the objects of family control. Also as expected, boys were found to be more delinquent than females.

The interesting aspect of Hagan's study, for present purposes, is his depiction of his male and female subjects. With females brought back into the picture, conformity is associated with the feminine rather than the masculine—for females are observed to be the more law-abiding sex. The problem that now arises is that Hirschi's control theory was developed with a male subject in mind. When applied to the female, it must surely produce curious results. How can the conforming female fit Hirschi's model of the dedicated breadwinner? Hagan's solution is simply to overlook Hirschi's version of conformity—as a responsible and commendable male activity—while adhering, nevertheless, to other parts of his control theory. Hagan describes law-abiding behaviour in the female in a manner more reminiscent of Parsons and Cohen than of Hirschi. Conformity becomes indisputably female in its symbolism, not male, and the effect is its instant devaluation.

Hagan's method of transmogrifying control theory is simple. He glamorises crime in the same fashion as criminologists outside the control school. Hagan suggests that 'it is useful to regard criminal and delinquent behaviour as pleasurable, if not liberating'. He explains: 'delinquency is frequently fun—and even more importantly, a type of fun infrequently allowed to females'. Whereas Hirschi's delinquents were a sorry lot, emotionally immature and indifferent to the needs of others, Hagan's delinquency 'involves a spirit of liberation, the opportunity to take risks, and a chance to pursue publicly some of the pleasures that are symbolic of adult male status outside the family'. Delinquency, to Hagan, is synonymous with 'independence and assertiveness' (Hagan et al., 1979:29).

The conforming female emerges, in Hagan's exposition, as a grey and lifeless creature. She is passive, compliant and dependent. Gone is Hirschi's rational and responsible agent, intelligently evaluating the risks and costs of crime. Conformity is now described as 'compliance'. The law-abiding female is biddable rather than responsible.

Hagan is thorough in his demolition of the agency of the female. Whereas Hirschi's conforming male was positively attached to conventional others and thus positively solicitous of their welfare, Hagan's female seems unable to construct complex and caring relationships, even with her mother who subjects her to her control. In Hagan's words, she is merely the 'object' of her mother's instrumental training to be compliant. Hagan is explicit about the status of the female as manipulated thing. He suggests that 'there may be reason to assume that women are oversocialised: more specifically, overcontrolled'. While males are encouraged to be independent and aggressive, to experiment with reckless pursuits, the female is steered into 'dependence, compliance and passivity' (Hagan et al., 1979:35).

Other empirical literature which has applied control theory to females is consistent with Hagan in its traditional depiction of the sexes. Hirschi's responsible and rational conforming person has been expunged in the translation of the theory to the female. One of the first attempts to hypothesise and test the relationship between the greater conformity of girls and the condition of being 'controlled' was made by Gary Jensen and Raymond Eve in 1964 and 1965 employing samples of American schoolchildren and a self-report delinquency test. They took the view that

> the sex differential is obviously compatible with a control perspective at the theoretical level. Compared to boys, girls are typically depicted as more closely bound to conventional persons, values, and institutions, and such sex differences in attachment, commitment, involvement, and belief should, according to control theory, lead to a sex differential in delinquent behaviour (Jensen and Eve, 1976:433).

Survey findings, however, did not unequivocally support this assertion. The various components of control theory were not able to account fully for the lesser involvement in delinquency reported by girls (depending on the seriousness of the offence, the male/female sex ratio varied from 1.6:1 to 6:1). Controlling for parental supervision, boys were still more delinquent than girls. The same was true for 'emotionally supportive parent–child relationships', attachment to the law, time spent on homework, school grades, and attachment to teachers and school. A combination of these factors when subjected to a multiple regression analysis, however, was able to reduce but not eliminate the sex differential of offending.

More promising results were obtained by Michael Hindelang (1973), several years later, when he attempted to replicate Hirschi's study using samples of American rural schoolboys and girls. Hindelang was able to establish substantial correspondence between his subjects' responses and the pioneer survey. Control theory was found to predict both male and female delinquency, although there was a tendency for relationships to be stronger with male subjects.

Adults were included in the sample employed by Douglas Smith in 1972 to investigate what he termed 'social bond' theory as an explanation of female crime (Smith, 1979). Framing his hypothesis around Durkheim's theory of social integration, rather than Hirschi's model of control, Smith questioned subjects about such social bonds as their number of children, the number of dwellings lived in, and their sense of belonging to their neighbourhood.

Notwithstanding the success of social bonding at predicting the variance in female criminality at least as well as the variance in male offending, controlling the factor of social bonds only slightly diminished the sex differential in offending observed by Smith. To clarify, even when females demonstrated weak social bonds they were still more conformist than males. Social bonds, therefore, were not sufficient to account for the greater conformity of females.

A partial test of Hirschi's control theory was undertaken more recently by Robert Mawby (1980) in one of the rare pieces of research making use of English subjects. Interested in the effect of attitudes toward police on subjects' propensity to engage in delinquency, Mawby asked schoolgirls and boys from Sheffield such questions as whether they felt most police did a good job and whether police were dishonest. As control theory predicts, the sex with the smallest involvement in delinquency, females, was significantly less cynical about police, believing them to be interested in helping them. As with previous inquiries, however, holding constant the social-bond variable of attitude towards police did not eliminate the sex differential of delinquency. Like Jensen and Eve, Mawby concluded that other factors must account for the greater conformity of girls.

A different slant on control theory's interpretation of the offending of girls was taken by four American criminologists. Flowing from their interest in the effects of masculine and feminine traits on the propensity to offend, Shover and associates (1979) determined to test also for Hirschi's elements of control: attachment (to parents and to school as well as parental control), commitment (to conventional educational and occupational goals), involvement (in conventional activities like homework) and belief (in the law). Thornton and James (1979) had previously tested for 'masculinity' of subjects and found that the presence of these characteristics had no effect on the frequency of the delinquency of girls. It is hardly surprising then that, when each of the social-bond variables was related to masculine expectations in girls, it did 'little to influence the original finding that masculine expectations are not related to delinquency among females' (Thornton and James, 1979:235).

Evidence of the effect of social bonding on the delinquency of girls, although of an indirect nature, can be gleaned, however, from a later report on this survey which also focused exclusively on the effects of masculinity on delinquency. While it was observed that the data 'provide no support for the hypothesis that masculinity is directly associated with females' delinquent activity' (Norland, Wessel and Shover, 1981:427), when 'attachment to conventional others' was included in the formula, masculine females reported more conventional attachments and this appeared to reduce their delinquency. The trouble with this finding, that social bonds exert a 'small, indirect effect' on the offending of girls, is that, as the authors themselves concede, the direction of the influence is the opposite of that expected. That is, control theory would predict that girls who are most like boys ('masculine' girls) would offend as much as boys because of a similarity of strength of social bonds—which should be weaker than those of more feminine, more conforming girls. However, the more masculine girls here were the most conventional in their attachments and consequently less delinquent.

In a further report on the same investigation, the relationship between masculinity theory, control theory and the delinquency of girls was theorised more explicitly (Shover et al., 1979). This was an attempt to make plain exactly what it is about being female that conduces to greater commitment to conventional others and therefore greater conformity. The approach adopted, not surprisingly, was along the lines of Hagan, with female conformity equated with lack of self-determination. From an early age, Shover argued, girls are touched, handled and talked to more than their brothers with a view to fostering their dependence. Girls are actively encouraged to find self-affirmation in the love and acceptance of others, while boys are rewarded for independent, objective achievements. A major consequence of girls being made subject to the reactions and opinions of others is their conformity. Put another way, boys are exhorted to be independent and accordingly their social bonds are weaker than, and their propensity for delinquency greater than, that of girls. Having theorised thus, Shover and colleagues predicted 'a positive relationship between traditional feminine expectations and belief in the validity of rules and law and a negative relationship between traditional masculine role expectations and the latter variable' (Shover et al., 1979:164–5).

Only the first part of the hypothesis was confirmed by the findings. These indicated that for both boys and girls traditional feminine expectations were positively related to a belief in the law as well as attachment to conventional others (teachers and mother). They also revealed that the more traditionally feminine the expectation, the less involved was the subject in property offences. Traditional male expectations, however, proved to be unimportant as indicators of the conventionality, or rather the unconventionality, of respondents.

Another interpretation of this research was mentioned earlier. Loy and Norland (1981) imposed concepts of androgyny, undifferentiated gender, traditional femininity and traditional masculinity on subjects' responses and discovered that undifferentiated females were the most delinquent girls. Employing these same concepts they also examined subjects' attitudes toward legal authority as well as their relationship with their mothers. Undifferentiated females were found to be less likely to respect the police than their traditional and androgynous counterparts and also less likely to identify closely with their mothers. Undifferentiated males, on the other hand, were the least delinquent boys. They were also more likely than other males to respect police and more likely to identify with their mothers.

It is unfortunate that the significance of these findings for either the masculinity hypothesis or control theory is not made plain. It was predicted that androgynous females would be the most delinquent because they would be the most like males. Instead it was observed that undifferentiated females engaged in the most delinquency and were the least bonded to conventional others through attitudes to the police and their mothers. The furthest that Loy and Norland are willing to venture about the meaning of these data is that the two variables of gender and social bonds are in some way related. They are quick to warn, however, that their concepts of 'androgyny' and 'undifferentiated gender' lack an informative 'theoretical meaning', that 'they represent nominal categories whose theoretical meaning is at best vague' (Loy and Norland, 1981:283).

Amalgamating the findings of these four reports on the one investigation, the implications for control theory as an explanation of female conformity are far from clear. Some conclusions though can be advanced. First, becoming more masculine does not weaken the social bonds of girls or conduce to delinquency (Thornton and James, 1979). On the contrary, masculinity seems to strengthen girls' conventional commitments and militate against delinquency (Norland, Wessel and Shover, 1981). A strong commitment to femininity, however, does seem to be related to stronger social bonds and greater conformity (Shover et al., 1979). Second, girls who are neither particularly feminine nor particular masculine in their expectations have the weakest social bonds among females and are the most delinquent (Loy and Norland, 1981). In sum, as girls move away from traditionally feminine expectations, but not necessarily towards masculine expectations, their social bonds weaken and their delinquency increases. It would seem, therefore, that feminine expectations at least partly account for female conformity in that they are associated with a tendency to greater commitment and attachment to conventional others.

Considered as a whole, the literature applying control theory to women is inconclusive. Ever since Hindelang discovered that the presence or absence of social bonds bore a weaker relation to female delinquency than to male delinquency—even though the correlation in the expected direction was apparent—criminologists have observed consistently that although the greater social bonding of girls goes some way to explain their greater conformity, it is not a sufficient explanation of the sex differential in offending.

Although there is considerable evidence of the greater 'bonding' of females to society, this has yet to be linked consistently with either femininity, as conventionally conceived, or to conformity. Certainly the commitments and concerns of girls designated 'masculine' throw this set of connections into question. Also challenging the logic of Hagan's version of the theory is the discovery that girls who embody neither male nor female stereotypes display the weakest social bonds. What this mixed bag of findings may suggest is that the traditional depictions of law-abiding women, à la Hagan, are misleading. They may indicate, instead, that the female subjects who have tended to confirm control theory are not the sort of passive, dependent and compliant women imagined by Hagan and his sympathisers. Instead, quite possibly, such women may be the more responsible, self-determining and rational persons to be found in Hirschi's original formulation.

The reconstruction of the law-abiding woman as agent instead of object makes sense, particularly when one is discussing research which replicated Hirschi's set of tests of control. If the male who is found to be committed to conventional activities and persons is depicted by Hirschi in terms of his rationality and calculation when it comes to the decision to obey the law, why should not the conforming female who displays similar conventional associations be depicted in like manner?

6

Crime and stigma

While it is possible to trace labelling theory as far back as Husserl (1859–1938), and his philosophy of phenomenology, within criminological circles the idea that external social stigmata or 'labels' make 'the criminal' is usually attributed to the American social scientist Howard Becker. It was the publication of *Outsiders* (1963) which launched labelling theory as a force in sociology and its subdiscipline, criminology. Here Becker examined the perceptions of jazz musicians as fringe members of society. He asserted that, although there was nothing intrinsically deviant about the life of a musician, conventional society labelled jazz players as bohemian and 'different' and, as a consequence, the musicians came to see themselves in this light. This feeling of difference then became a positive force for solidarity among the musicians, entrenching their deviance.

The essence of labelling theory is simply this process of the application and receipt of deviant labels. It considers how the powerful members of society, 'moral entrepreneurs', make labels (such as 'criminal' or 'bohemian') and apply them with such efficacy to the powerless that the latter internalise the message and reconstruct their self-image and behaviour accordingly. In other words, it is a matter of 'giving a dog a bad name'.

A deliberate thrust of the new 'labelling' approach, said Becker, was to develop an affinity with the subject and present 'his' perceptions of his deviance. For this reason, the labelling school has sometimes been referred to as 'underdog sociology'. It is about giving the weaker members of society, those susceptible to labelling, a voice. The method advanced by Becker to uncover the deviant view was field research which required participant observation. The sociologist who wished to pursue the labelling approach, according to Becker, was obliged to make the moral decision of taking part in activities which society regarded as bad or even criminal. The fieldworker had to participate with the deviant in the deviant's activities.

In the case of the dance or jazz musician, a central concern of *Outsiders*, Becker was in an ideal position to develop rapport with his subjects because he was one of them. Becker tells his reader that '[a]t the time I made the study I had played the piano professionally for several years and was active in musical circles in Chicago'. Indeed Becker was so much at home with his subject that he did not find it necessary to search out musicians or to construct questionnaires to elicit their views. Instead Becker was in their midst, living and breathing the life of the musician. 'Most of my observations,' he says, 'were carried out on the job, and even on the stand as we played' (Becker, 1963:84).

The brief of this volume is to discern depictions of men and women in criminology. How did Becker perceive the sexes? Although there is the occasional reference to female singers in *Outsiders*, Becker's musicians are on the whole unmistakably male. The sex of his subject becomes manifest when one discovers half a chapter devoted to the effect of 'parents and wives' (not husbands) on the lives of his musicians. Becker is tacitly approving of his male musicians throughout his work. He is overtly laudatory, however, in a chapter which gives an account of the 'culture' of the dance musician. It is largely a glamorous and appealing life, says Becker. 'The musician,' he tells us, 'is conceived of as an artist who possesses a mysterious artistic gift setting him apart from all other people.' In the world of the musician there are two types of people: there are musicians and there are 'squares'. The musician embodies the desirable qualities; the square represents 'the opposite of that valued by musicians' (Becker, 1963:85).

'Musicians live an exotic life,' opines one of their number. It is 'like living in a jungle or something'. Some players are of the view 'that only musicians are sensitive and unconventional enough to be able to give sexual satisfaction to a woman'. Becker does not refute this suggestion. The musician values 'devil-may-care activities'. No one can tell him what to do: 'behaviour which flouts conventional social norms is greatly admired.' In fact 'the crazier a guy acts, the greater he is, the more everyone likes him' (Becker, 1963:86–7).

Who then is the square? The squares who feature prominently in the lives of musicians are paying customers who exercise an unwanted influence over the musician. Squares are also families and in particular wives who appear to have little say in the life of the dedicated musician. The square is uninteresting, insensitive, laughable and ludicrous. The square 'lacks this special gift and any understanding of the music or the way of life of those who possess it'. The square is ignorant and intolerant, a person to be feared when he is a customer who, literally, calls the tune. When she is a wife, the square is relatively powerless but can still dampen the *joi de vivre* of her musician husband. The 'wife' abides by social conventions which the musician refuses to acknowledge. The 'wife' endeavours to tie down her husband, to make him responsible. Becker's sympathies as a musician himself are not with her. She is a spoilsport; she threatens to turn this colourful creature into a 'non-musician', 'a companion and provider'. Becker cites a musical colleague on the appropriate place of the wife: 'Hell, I like the business too much, I'm not gonna put it down for her or any woman' (Becker, 1963:89, 116–17).

Another conversation between musicians documented by Becker illustrates the plight of being subordinated by a wife. Gene, a drummer, observes that 'Course, his wife wanted him to get out of the business . . . [But] he'd rather be playing and it's a drag to him to have that fucking day job so why should he hold on to it?' Johnny, the saxophonist, replies: 'You know why, because his wife makes him hold on to it.' Gene responds: 'He shouldn't let her boss him around like that. For Christ sake, my old lady don't tell me what to do. He shouldn't put up with that crap.' The denouement, apparently a happy ending, is that the subject of the conversation is wooed away from his day job and returns to his music (Becker, 1963:118).

The disdain for the musician's wife, who threatens to break the spirit of her husband, does not mean that women who themselves become musicians are held in any higher regard. The few insights we are allowed into the role of the woman in musical circles suggests that her exclusive function is that of sexual object. She is not to be accepted as part of the musical 'fraternity'. Musicians perceive her as a foil, an inauthentic artist, rather than as a serious musical partner.

> Eddie: Well, you could have a sexy little bitch to stand up in front and sing and shake her ass at the bears [squares]. Then you could get a job. And you could still play great when she wasn't singing.
> Charlie: Well, wasn't that what Q——'s band was like? Did you enjoy that? Did you like the way she sang?
> Eddie: No, man, but we played jazz, you know (Becker, 1963:93).

The portrayal of women in Becker's *Outsiders* is uniformly an unattractive one. Their principal role is that of the 'square' wife of the musician; she represents the other side—the conventional order which threatens to destroy all talent and imagination. Becker's sympathetic portraits derived from careful participant-observation are reserved for the male musician. At no time does he display empathy or rapport for his female subjects. The voice or perspective of the woman as musician or as wife of musician is entirely absent. She is viewed at all times through the unsympathetic eyes of Becker and his fellow musicians. As wife, she is invariably colourless and conformist. Her husband, by contrast, is 'spontaneous' and 'individualistic'. Her sole preoccupation appears to be to expunge these characteristics and to drag her partner down to her own level.

LABELLING AND WOMEN

When it came to the application of labelling theory to women, two approaches were open to criminologists. One was to employ the sort of close observation used by Becker on his male musicians to develop accounts of the interior lives of women. The other was to adopt Becker's attitude to women: to depict them as clinging to conventional society—inert, colour-less and unattractive. The few endeavours to use labelling theory with women have taken the latter course.

In 1977, the American criminologist Anthony Harris theor-ised the greater conformity of females in terms of their ma-nipulation by powerful men who convince them that crime is a wholly inappropriate activity for women. Why these powerful men want women law-abiding is that women perform vital social functions—those of child-rearing and home-making. Women would be unable to perform these functions if they were sent to prison. And if no one were home looking after the children, the 'institutional hegemony of the socially dominant' would be threatened by the possibility of the break-up of the nuclear family. Black, ghetto males, on the other hand, are dispensable. They can be sacrificed to the criminal justice system because their imprisonment represents no real loss to their families: 'the vacated role will presumably be filled easily by the black women' (Harris, 1977:13). Nor are they any loss to the economy since, chances are, they are unemployed.

How the 'institutional hegemony' manages to ensure that the indispensable (women as home-makers) remain law-abiding while the dispensable (unemployed, black males) fill the prisons is by fostering an image of the criminal type which fits the socio-economic and physical characteristics of the latter group and positively excludes the former. In other words, 'dominant typifi-cations about what kinds of actors "do" criminal behaviour . . . have played a crucial . . . role in . . . keeping men in crime and women out of it' (Harris, 1977:15). Women do not offend or do not appear to offend as much as men because the 'type-scripts' of the sort of people who act in roles of criminals dictate that the actor be male.

Harris is clear that his is an extension of, and an improvement on, labelling theory, not a new and independent model of crime causation. But whereas mainstream labelling theorists declare that it is when the powerful label the powerless as deviant or criminal that the latter assumes a deviant self-evaluation, Harris focuses on an earlier stage in the process of criminogenesis. Official labelling is not vital to Harris' model because he be-lieves that the powerful make so widely known their idea of criminal and non-criminal types that those who are 'scripted' as criminals assume the role even before they come into contact with law enforcement agencies.

Although not explicit in her debt to labelling theory, Greer Litton Fox (1977) presents another interpretation of female conformity employing the idea that women are controlled by social constructs of appropriate feminine behaviour. In Fox's version of labelling theory, women choose not to offend for two reasons. The criminal label is too costly for them: 'The message in literature is unfailingly clear: misfortune, misery, and public ostracism are the lot of the fallen woman' (Fox, 1977:807). More positively, women obey the law because social-value constructs such as 'good girl', 'lady' and 'nice girl' exhort them to be model citizens or risk negative social evaluation.

As with Harris' model of deviant type-scripts, Fox's 'nice girl' construct does not depend for its efficacy on acts of labelling women as 'good' or 'bad' by external agents of control. Women are controlled, instead, by society's willingness to withdraw the 'good girl' label for the slightest infraction. Theirs is a lifelong quest for the 'good girl' label and avoidance of the 'bad girl' construct. Where Fox clearly dissents from Becker is that Becker conceives of people as free to pursue their own desires until they are confronted with a criminal label. A negative and deviant self-image may then be acquired and a deviant way of life entrenched. It is Fox's view that women do not even have this 'pre-labelling' freedom accorded men: 'There is no front stage/back stage dichotomy . . . women are "on" whenever and wherever they are, whether in the company of men, strangers, or other women' (Fox, 1977:811). Women are not considered 'nice' until labelled otherwise. Rather, the prized 'nice girl' label is something to be striven for at all times. Wherever she is, a woman must positively prove she is a lady. Her status as a 'nice girl' is in constant jeopardy and this threatened loss is sufficient to keep her behaving in a conventional, conformist way most of the time.

The idea that official criminal labelling is reserved for men because women can be kept conformist in this sort of informal and subtle way also underpins the thinking of Hagan, Simpson and Gillis (1979) whose research was outlined in the previous chapter. Hagan and his associates maintain that the stigma of the criminal label is used in the public sphere to deal only with the criminality of men. Females are accorded different treatment. They are kept in line by informal mechanisms, in particular the exhortations of family members (mainly their mothers) to confine themselves to the private sphere of the home and be dependent, compliant and passive.

A further reason for the different criminal labelling of boys and girls has recently been suggested by Darrell Steffensmeier and John Kramer (1980). By investigating levels of stigmatisation of samples of convicted female and male felons, they found that males were victimised to a greater extent. This they attributed to 'fear of the male offender and naivete concerning the female offender'. To clarify:

> Because of the definitions surrounding the male role (the greater aggressiveness and autonomy) and because of the greater physical strength of the male, the male felon is seen as being more capable and more likely to use force, to harm or threaten someone, that is, as being more dangerous than his female counterpart (Steffensmeier and Kramer, 1980:7).

In describing attitudes toward the female offender as naive, Steffensmeier and Kramer mean that women are seen as less capable of serious criminal action and as less responsible for their behaviour than men.

CRITIQUE

The central problem with labelling theory in its application to women is the way it has been used to stereotype and devalue its subject. An approach to social behaviour explicitly designed to imbue the individual with rationality, with a sense of subjective intention and purpose, perversely, has expunged the agency of the female.

Howard Becker's aim in advancing labelling theory was to acknowledge the point of view of the deviant. In Becker's assessment, the criminological subject exercised a degree of control over his life hitherto unrecognised by the discipline. From the outset Becker maintained that he was dealing with intelligent people whose behaviour was not simply a matter of social engineering. Becker's jazz musicians could question the rules applied to them by the conventional order and condemn those who judged them as incompetent to do so.

Becker's research methods were designed to allow the deviant actor to give expression to his view of the world. The extensive extracts from conversations between musicians in *Outsiders* credit them with an understanding of their situation. Becker believed that his jazz musicians possessed insights which not only could assist the criminologist in explaining deviant behaviour but could also highlight the hypocrisies and deficiencies of the justice system.

In its female version, labelling theory seems to have lost sight of the deviant as actor and as social critic. Criminologists interested in women have rarely approached their subjects for their account of their experience. They appear thus to have assumed that women are unable to shed light on the reasons for their own actions. They possess no critical insights. Pity rather than empathy characterises the new work on women. The female subject of the labelling school is neither a glamorous nor impressive character. Stripped of any ability to challenge or question her position in society, she is conceived as object rather than agent.

There are other problems with the labelling theory of female conformity which concern its lack of theoretical precision and sustained empirical testing. The two most thorough expositions of the theory, those of Harris and Fox, are also the most vague in the constructs they employ. These authors also make no attempt to verify their ideas.

Reducing Harris' theory to its bare essentials, we have the proposition that because the powerful in society (who are men) prefer women to be home acting as the bedrock of the nuclear family, they (powerful men) popularise stereotypes of criminals which are so at odds with the feminine ideal that most women cannot conceive of themselves offending. Why it is in the interests of the powerful to foster any 'type-scripts' of offenders at all is not clear. For if crime can be eliminated simply by defining it as inappropriate for certain types of people, why not make it inappropriate for all types? If the solution to crime were really this simple criminology would be surely, by now, a redundant discipline.

Another problem with Harris' formulation is that it is difficult to imagine how it could be tested. Certainly Harris makes no attempt to do this. Nor does he offer any suggestions indicating how it might be done. Would it involve black, unemployed male offenders being asked whether they offended because they are unemployed, black and male? And how would the researcher cope with such anomalies as the white, middle-class housewife who commits a serious theft?

Finally, Harris' model seems to be based on circular reasoning; in fact it is almost a tautology. Harris maintains that women do not offend because there are no stereotypes, models or type-scripts into which they can cast themselves. And working-class, black males do offend because they know full well that other working-class, black males fill the courts and prisons. Surely all this is saying is that women do not offend because women do not offend. And poor, black males do offend because poor, black males offend. If this interpretation of Harris' reasoning is correct, the concept of the deviant type-script does not appear to be very helpful. If, on the other hand, Harris is wishing to take his theory beyond this tautology by examining the socioeconomic and political structures in society which conduce to a small minority having sufficient power to channel certain groups into certain forms of behaviour, and others into others (an interpretation not incompatible with his theory of deviant typescripts), he fails to do so here.

Although Fox's model does not seem to suffer from this circularity of reasoning, it, too, appears to be more descriptive than explanatory. Women do not offend because they are taught to be 'good girls' and are powerfully stigmatised for deviation from this stereotype. Women are conformist because they are more effectively restricted and hence forced to be conformist. But again the more fundamental question is begged: why should women and not men be singled out for such successful socialisation into conformity? Harris suggests that society has a stake in keeping women in the home, as housewives and as mothers. A more detailed analysis of the functions served by gender roles, however, would seem to be needed here. And again, if society already knows how to achieve a crime-free citizenry—socialise people to be 'nice'—why isn't everyone taught to be 'nice', thereby eliminating crime and social disorder? Perhaps, it can be argued, such selective socialisation is a function of competitive, capitalist societies being unable to afford too many people with such passive and accommodating characteristics. Unfortunately, Fox does not explore the politics underlying such discrimination.

A further flaw in Fox's theory concerns her belief that women are more seriously stigmatised than men for any form of deviance. Employing Becker's reasoning, the greater the stigma, the more the victim of labelling will internalise this negative evaluation and consequently turn to more serious forms of deviance. It follows that if women are stigmatised more than men when they break the law, they are also more likely than men to become serious habitual criminals. But this is simply not the case. The fact that women are in the main, and far more so than men, first known offenders would suggest either than women are not subject to the same degree of labelling as men or that, if they are, it does not have the same effect on them. For after women come before a court they tend not to reoffend. Fox might respond to this by claiming that the overarching requirement to be a 'lady' keeps the vast majority of women on the straight and narrow so that they never attract a criminal label. But this does not help to explain the behaviour of that small minority of women who do offend. These women who are officially designated 'criminal' must realise that they have fallen short of the 'nice girl' model. A negative and criminal self-image should result, entrenching deviance and conducing to further offending. But the statistics on the recidivism of men and women reveal that it is mainly men who reoffend.

At least a partial solution to this dilemma is provided by Hagan (1979) and by Steffensmeier and Kramer (1980). It is Hagan's view that social control is sexually stratified so that the official criminal label is reserved for men while informal familial controls are used for errant females—even when they engage in crime. Steffensmeier and Kramer, too, feel that when women offend they are not stigmatised to the same extent as men because women are perceived as neither threatening nor dangerous. Although this view of labelling seems to contradict Fox's, the two perhaps can be reconciled by maintaining that, although women are encouraged to perceive the consequences of deviance as dire (which manages to keep most of them law-abiding), those few who offend nevertheless, in practice, are not treated as dangerous villains. Instead, the 'nice girl' construct persists so that errant females are soon guided back to the informal controls of the family—their criminality viewed as an aberration—and the admonitions to be a lady return with even greater force. It is pertinent to note here that the few women who end up in prison, where one could reason that criminal stigmatisation would be at its worst, tend not to be treated as failed women, beyond redemption. Instead, the strength of the 'nice girl' construct is manifest, with prison staff encouraging prisoners to use cosmetics, to groom themselves and to acquire domestic, as opposed to vocational, skills (Smart, 1976:140–5).

Although theirs is a more explicitly feminist perspective, the American criminologists Klein and Kress (1976) also advance a theory to explain why, for certain crimes, women may not be subject to the same labelling as men. According to Klein and Kress, whereas women who are construed as sexual offenders are probably treated more punitively by the agents of the law for jeopardising their socially prescribed reproductive function, women who engage in property crimes are treated more leniently. The reason is that women are perceived as economically marginal and docile and, as such, their non-sexual offending is not regarded as a serious threat to the social order.

Notwithstanding the efforts of feminist criminologists such as Klein and Kress to provide a more sympathetic treatment of the economic and social plight of the deviant woman, the image of the 'other' sex first presented by Becker in *Outsiders* remains largely unchallenged. Women are tied to the conventional order: they are passive, compliant and dependent on social approval. Missing from the labelling literature are detailed accounts of the female experience which endeavour to invest women with a sense of intention and purpose. Criminologists have not endeavoured to replicate the sort of research based on participant-observation employed by Becker to present the perspective of his male musicians. Neither the criminal nor conforming woman has been given such a voice: the opportunity to say in her own words how she perceives her own social reality. The effect has been to strip her of all intelligence, wit or charm. Even those criminologists concerned about the position of the 'marginalised' female have failed to construct an alternative and more flattering view of their subject.

The observations of Jean Anyon (1983) on the problems of socialisation theory are pertinent in the present context. Anyon maintains that suggestions such as those of Harris and Fox that women are fully constrained and managed by powerful gender-role training ignores the social reality that women are not quite so submissive. Although Anyon sees value in the socialisation argument, that women are taught to behave in a passive manner and to depend on male opinion, she claims that socialisation is not as successful as writers such as Fox would have us believe. While women often do behave in accepted ways, she says that they rarely accede fully to the demands of their gender role. Anyon's description of the response of women to society's training is 'a simultaneous process of accommodation and resistance' (Anyon, 1983:19). The accommodating female is depicted vividly in criminological accounts which invoke labelling theory. No time is given, however, to the female who resists the gender stereotype.

The self-determination and purpose of Becker's offender continue to be seen as inapplicable to women. Harris and Fox, key proponents of the theory for women, both maintain that official criminal labelling is not needed to control the behaviour of the female. For women are controlled well before they attract criminal epithets. Harris' 'type-script' of the offender and Fox's 'good girl' construct depict women as either fully constrained from offending by the conspicuous masculinity of powerful stereotypes of criminals or as compelled to be conformist by society's normative restrictions and exhortations to be 'nice'. Indeed Fox is explicit about the completeness of society's control over women using the 'nice girl' construct. She feels that women are required to be good wherever they are—'in the company of men, strangers, or other women' (Fox, 1977:811). There is no room here for the sort of individualism and glamour described by Becker when the male was the subject of interpretation. Nor is there room for the woman who casts a critical eye on her gender role and who refuses to submit to all its requirements. While labelling theorists may be right in claiming that men have more freedom than women to deviate, they have developed their arguments about the socialised woman to a point at which her humanity has been extinguished.

7

The women's liberation thesis

Since 1975, the impact of the women's liberation movement on female crime has become the basis of a heated debate in the criminological literature on women. The catalyst was Freda Adler's *Sisters in Crime* (1975) in which the proposition was advanced that women's liberation was causing women to engage in more violent crime. In an oft-cited passage of this work, Adler put her thesis in vigorous and colourful terms: 'Like her legitimate based sister, the female criminal knows too much to pretend, or return to her former role as a second-rate criminal confined to "feminine" crimes such as shoplifting and prostitution' (Adler, 1975:15).

To Adler, the liberation of women in western society is a *fait accompli*. Women have fought and won their battle for equality. They have 'come of age', and 'the phenomenon of female criminality is but one wave in this rising tide of female assertiveness' (Adler, 1975:1).

That women criminals today represent a 'new breed' can be demonstrated, argues Adler, by evidence of the changing nature of female involvement in a wide variety of crimes. About prostitutes, Adler asserts that they are no longer the passive objects of male needs: 'Like other modern women, today's prostitute is better educated, better accepted, and more independent of men.' As illegal drug takers, women 'have shed much of their reluctance to pursue sources of supply into illicit channels, and they are becoming as eager as males to reach out for thrills rather than just relief'. A further example of the burgeoning of female crime involves the white-collar worker. Women in the workforce are no longer 'token females' or 'window dressing'. They are now 'socially climbing up the business ladder' and making use of their 'vocational liberation' to pursue careers in white-collar crime (Adler, 1975:83, 123, 167).

Evidence that 'liberation' is causing women to engage in more crime, according to Adler, is provided by the official crime statistics on the sex ratio of black offenders. Adler's claim is that this ratio has always tended to be smaller than that for white criminals (meaning a greater involvement of black women in crime) because 'in a grimly sardonic sense the black female has been "liberated" for over a century'. Often the sole breadwinner for her family, the black woman's lot in America has not been a happy one. But it has at least made her independent: 'Aggressiveness, toughness, and a certain street-wise self-sufficiency were just a few of the characteristics necessary for the black woman to shepherd her beleaguered flock of children, siblings, and consorts through the wastelands of educational, social, financial and cultural deprivations' (Adler, 1975: 140, 142).

In *Sisters in Crime*, Adler's lengthy analysis of the nature of the new female criminal seems to rest on two points. One is that women's liberation has brought out women's competitive instincts. Women are now more assertive, more aggressive and, indeed, more 'masculine'. Her other argument is that women's liberation has opened up structural opportunities for women to offend. For example, women now have more opportunities to engage in crime in the workplace.

Central to Adler's thesis is an assumption that crime is a male activity which is therefore appealing and prestigious. It is axiomatic, to Adler, that women would want to emulate men, even when they commit crime. In maintaining that the female is no longer to be regarded as a 'second-rate criminal' Adler seeks to elevate the criminal woman to the status of the male. Female offending, she insists, is every bit as assertive, thrilling and cunning as that of men.

The crucial point about Adler's description of crime, for current purposes, is her acceptance of traditional criminology's conception of crime as an expression of masculinity. Without reservation, Adler endorses a view of offending to be found in the work of criminologists of the forties and fifties—such as Cohen and Sutherland. Adler builds her thesis of 'the new female criminal' on old foundations: its first premise is that crime is a vehicle for exhibiting traditional masculine qualities and hence, as Hagan has put it, it is fun, it involves a spirit of liberation, of risk-taking.

For women 'to get in on the action', they too must behave like men, declares Adler. They must become competitive, defiant and daring. Then they too can take their place as fully liberated felons. Crime is an appealing pursuit because it has been the province of the male. But women now can show their flair, their toughness and their independence by becoming criminals too. This is a significant achievement of the women's movement: liberation has meant that women now can compete successfully with men in both the 'straight' and 'criminal' world.

Three standard criminological ideas are employed and re-inforced in Adler's work. One is of the male representing the qualities of toughness, verve and intrepidity. The second is of crime as a symbolically masculine activity which thus embodies these attractive male attributes. The third is of a domesticated female character (the pre-liberated woman) whose conformity is inert and uninteresting (but who, in Adler's account, blossoms when she imitates the male and turns to crime). These three depictions, which we have seen repeated in each of the criminological approaches considered here, are all implicit in Adler's argument that 'liberated' women are now assuming the more attractive, though violent and anti-social, characteristics of the male.

Since 1975, when Adler published *Sisters in Crime*, there has been a steady stream of replies to her thesis of the new female criminal. Feminists in particular have been prominent in this riposte. Their commentaries on Adler's theory have consistently shown a spirit of scepticism for her entire set of proposals about the nature of crime, the nature of men and the nature of women.

The first and perhaps most fundamental objection to Adler

has been her use of statistics. Adler, her critics allege, provides the most meagre evidence of her female crime wave. Those figures she employs depend on statistical techniques which have since been denounced. Adler's critics are particularly scathing of her use of percentage increases to establish her case of the new female criminal.

A handicap to the criminologist wishing to determine the nature of female crime is the numbers involved. According to official statistics, women represent as little as 2–3 per cent of persons committing violent offences such as robbery or burglary. The problems of the smallness of the officially recognised female offender population in many categories of crime are various. One major problem is well demonstrated by Adler's work, as her critics have been quick to remark. It involves the construction of large trends out of small increases in the number of offenders using percentages. Drawing from the FBI Uniform Crime Reports Adler contends that

> During the twelve-year period between 1960 and 1972 the number of women arrested for robbery rose by 277 %, while the male figure rose 69 %. Dramatic differences are found in embezzlement (up 280 % for women, 50 % for men), larceny (up 303 % for women, 82 % for men), and burglary (up 168 % for women, 63 % for men) (Adler, 1975:16, 17).

It is percentage increases like these that lead Adler to conclude that there has been a burgeoning of female crime.

It is not difficult to refute the argument that violent female crime has mushroomed. As Carol Smart (1979) observes in her critique of 'the new female criminal', the theory is based on a statistical illusion caused by the smallness of the base. Closer scrutiny of the crime statistics reveals that the absolute number of women involved in the new wave of violent female crime remains small, though not insignificant. Employing the statistics of the British Home Office, Smart examines female crime trends from 1965 to 1975 and finds an increase of 225 per cent in violent offences against the person. She then examines the absolute number of women involved and finds that they represent only a handful of offenders: 'For example, between 1965 and 1975 there has been an increase of 500% in murder by women; the absolute figure for 1965 was one and for 1975 it was five' (Smart, 1979:53).

Another criminologist concerned about the way that percentage increases have been used to generate alarm over increases in certain female crimes is Laura Crites (1976). Like Smart, Crites quickly disposes of Adler's argument with some simple calculations, this time employing the Uniform Crime Reports:

> 1974 statistics show a 450% increase in arrests of adolescent females for negligent manslaughter compared with a 36% drop for young males. This figure is much less sensational, however, when one sees that it results from an increase from two females arrested in 1960 to eleven arrested throughout the United States in 1974 (Crites, 1976:33).

Crites concludes that one 'would not point to these eleven as proof of a trend toward violence on the part of young females'. And yet this is precisely what Adler has done.

More fundamentally, critics of Adler maintain that most of the assumptions upon which her thesis is based are wrong. It is said that female criminals are not competitive, masculine and aggressive. Nor have women achieved equality with men. Before examining more closely these other challenges to Adler's 'new female criminal', a variant of the women's liberation thesis developed contemporaneously by another American criminologist requires some attention. This is Rita James Simon's (1975) idea that the women's movement influenced female crime in two ways: it caused an increase in property crime and it reduced the violent offending of women.

Simon argues that increased occupational opportunities for women, flowing from their 'liberation', mean that they now have more occasion to commit crimes against property. Hence female property crime has flourished. Improved vocational opportunities for women has had a second pronounced effect on their behaviour. It has diminished the frustrations of the stifling and unsatisfying role of housewife. This diminution of tension has had the beneficial effect of reducing the likelihood of women being violent towards their loved ones.

For all that Simon maintains that women's perceptions of

their increased opportunities have reshaped their offending, she does not believe that female criminals today are self-consciously and actively competing with men. She is therefore clearly at variance with Adler when she maintains that 'given the characteristics of the members of the women's movement, it is unlikely that it has had a significant impact or . . . indeed that it has made much of an impression on women already involved in crime. Indeed, most of these women have yet to hear of consciousness raising, and of sisterhood in a political sense' (Simon, 1975:18). Whereas Adler contends that women are becoming more violent, Simon takes the opposite view. This does not mean that she attempts to verify empirically her proposition that women now experience less frustration with their role because of greater occupational opportunities. Nor does she try to prove that there is any causal relationship between these diminished frustrations and what is posed as the lesser violence of criminal women.

What Simon does attempt to test empirically is whether women's occupational opportunities have already increased by examining the demographic characteristics of American women. In fact Simon devotes an entire chapter of *Women and Crime* to considering changes in women's participation in the labour force and concludes that 'the picture that emerges from these statistics about the current status of the American woman is not radically different from the picture that could have been drawn one or even two decades ago'. It is odd, therefore, that in spite of this finding Simon proceeds to theorise later in her volume that women's increased involvement in property crimes is a function of changes in their contribution to the labour force and more specifically that 'in the past their opportunities have been much more limited' (Simon, 1975:29, 47).

The conflation in the literature of the main issues in the women's liberation debate makes it necessary to isolate and analyse each strand of the polemic before undertaking any useful critique. Given significant points of divergence in the theses of Adler and Simon, it is important to note, from the outset, that there is not a clear and consistent theory of the relationship between women's liberation and the nature of female crime. Nevertheless, it is possible to identify several key arguments. First, the liberation movement is responsible for an increase in female crime (the thesis of both Adler and Simon). While Adler maintains that female offending has increased across the board, and that it is more violent than before the movement, Simon claims that only female property crime has increased and that women are tending to become less violent. Second, the increment in female crime is a function of women becoming more masculine. Gender roles have begun to converge and women are therefore more aggressive and assertive (Adler's theory). The greater volume of female crime is also a result of increased opportunities to offend because of increasing equality in the workplace (Adler believes women are now equal; Simon asserts that so far the changes have been minor). Finally, the supposed increases in female offending can be attributed to women becoming actively competitive with men as they absorb, either consciously (Adler) or unconsciously (Simon), the rhetoric of the women's movement. Simon's theory that women are becoming less violent hinges on the argument that more options in the workplace should lessen the frustrations inherent in the role of housewife and diminish the violence of female offenders.

Despite some alarming reports in newspapers about female crime waves, the bulk of research conducted since *Sisters in Crime* has revealed consistently that any substantial increases in the contribution of women to the total volume of crime have been confined to the category of property offending, mainly of a petty nature (Smith and Visher, 1980; Box, 1983:195). Adler's theory of the new violent, female offender can be dismissed. Women are not catching up with men as violent criminals; they are not taking over the domain of violent crime.

Simon's notion that changing structural opportunities for women have reduced any female tendencies to violence can be similarly dealt with by a brief look at the statistics. Simon anticipates a diminution of violent, female crime as women's occupational opportunities unfold. And yet she herself concedes that over the two decades she considers (1953 to 1972), the contribution of women to the total crime figure has remained stable. Simon's theory that women are already experiencing less frustration and therefore tending to become less violent does not find support in these statistics.

The second proposition identified above, that women have become more masculine, and that this is reflected in their offending, can also be quickly dealt with. The review of the literature on masculinity theory conducted earlier revealed that criminologists have had little success at uncovering a relationship between masculinity in females and their criminality. 'Masculine' females do not engage in more crime than 'unmasculine' females. Instead, there is a tendency for masculine females to display concern for conventional persons and to have conventional associations. So whether or not the women's movement is making females more like males, and this has yet to be established, this masculinisation does not seem to be conducive to offending.

One way of testing the contention that substantial increases in female crime—and as we have seen, these are confined to crimes against property—are the result of improved occupational opportunities, is to examine the demographic characteristics of women criminals. Such an analysis has already been conducted by Laura Crites (1976). In 1976 she studied the socioeconomic and racial characteristics of American female offenders. She discovered that most were from minority racial groups, were employed in poorly paid and low-status jobs, and were undereducated. Crites concluded that the typical female offender was not a recipient of the benefits of the women's movement, that 'employment benefits derived from the feminist push for equal employment opportunities accrue predominantly to white, middle-class females' (Crites, 1973:36).

What the thesis of the new white-collar female criminal overlooks is that increases in female crime have not been in the business area. Instead, they have been, in the main, confined to the offence of shoplifting. More particularly, the burgeoning of female store theft has involved larcenies of a trivial nature (in the value of the item stolen) typified by their amateurishness: the vast majority of female shoplifters are first offenders who use unsophisticated methods to conceal and remove goods from stores (Cameron, 1964; Brady and Mitchell,

1971; Naffin, 1983: Chapter 4). As Crites puts it, the crimes of women 'continue to mirror their traditional role in society' (Crites, 1976:38).

In line with Crites (as well as Simon in parts of *Women and Crime*), another American criminologist, Darrell Steffensmeier, believes that the women's movement has not opened up illegitimate opportunities in the workplace for the simple reason that women are still employed in the same traditionally female jobs. Speaking of the American experience, Steffensmeier cites labour force statistics which show women still concentrated in a narrow range of occupations: teaching, clerical, service and retail sales work. He concludes that 'from at least the early sixties . . . women have made few gains in terms of the occupational distribution, the relative earnings of men and women, or in terms of the pattern of women's participation in the labour force with respect to age and life cycle' (Steffensmeier, 1980:1100). Labour statistics for Australia confirm that here, too, women are still mostly employed in only a narrow range of jobs.[1]

Another recent endeavour to quash the notion that female offenders are liberated women who have moved into the male occupational sphere is that of Jane Roberts Chapman (1980). Remarking on the paucity of data on the socioeconomic status of women criminals, Chapman made her own inquiry into the criminal effects of women's involvement in the labour force. She compared the United States' figures for women's labour-force participation from 1930 to 1970 with the number of female arrests for the same period. Her findings were as follows: first, women arrested were 'an extremely small element' of the female population compared with the number of working women expressed as a percentage of the population. Second, arrests rose more than labour-force participation (and therefore it could be argued that female crime was the result of a greater demand for employment than the number of jobs available). And third, the smallest increases in arrests coincided with those periods of the greatest increase in economic activity.

In conjunction, these findings would seem to support a theory of the relationship between employment and crime diametrically opposed to that offered by the women's liberation thesis. The absence, rather than the availability, of employment opportunity for women seems to lead to increases in female crime, for when times are good, the offending of women stabilises rather than escalates.

An explanation of data such as these has been developed by feminist criminologist Carol Smart (1979) in yet another attempt to debunk the 'myth' of the new female criminal. Smart first establishes the foundations for her theory by suggesting that any improvements in the labour market generated by the women's movement have been limited to middle-class positions and are therefore unlikely to have had any effect on the uneducated, working-class, female offender. Like Crites, Smart observes that if women criminals are employed at all, they are likely to be engaged in unskilled manual labour. And this represents no change at all, for 'working-class women have always worked outside the home: this is not an achievement of a relatively recent women's movement' (Smart, 1979:57). The real relationship between changing occupational patterns and female crime, suggests Smart, is the reverse of the Adler/Simon thesis. Submitting evidence of a worsening occupational position for women,[2] she suggests that they are increasingly being channelled into poorly paid, unrewarding and insecure work at a time when the economy is in a state of decline. Smart advocates an alternative line of inquiry into the effect of the labour market on female crime. Redundancy, unemployment and monotonous, unskilled and low-paid work should all be examined as factors contributing to women's propensity to offend. With this suggestion Adler's theory of the new female criminal is not only rejected but turned on its head to reveal a potentially more fruitful field of inquiry. The growth of female shoplifting may be explained by greater financial pressures experienced by working-class women who, finding themselves redundant, turn to petty theft to alleviate economic strain.

In the writing of feminists such as Smart, Chapman and Crites one can discern the beginnings of a fundamentally new approach to the study of women and crime. This approach is remarkable in several ways. It contains an implicit criticism of the tendency to regard crime as prestigious—so central to the work of criminologists from the fifties (witness Cohen) to the seventies (Hagan). It entails an implicit rejection of theories which reduce crime to a simple expression of gender, ignoring the less palatable facts about the social need behind much offending. Thus it challenges the traditional assessment of women's lives, as protected from economic concerns in the cloistered domestic sphere, and seeks to bring into discussion some concrete facts about the female experience. It recognises that women are exposed to the pressures of the public world in quite untraditional and unfeminine ways: they suffer unemployment and they have real financial problems.

The feminists' scepticism about Adler's thesis, their implicit wish to debunk the glamour she invests in male crime, has led to a new form of social realism in the study of the female criminal. The plight of the woman obliged to steal because of real economic hardship is unenviable. Confronted by chronic economic difficulties it is unlikely, say the feminists, that the criminal woman is either manifesting her gender-role concerns, as she shoplifts, or seeking to compete with the criminal male. More probable, they say, is that her stealing has a straight-forward, rational motive of filling a material need.

The idea that women's 'economic marginalisation', rather than the creation of employment opportunities, has contributed to female property offending has been advanced more recently by British criminologists Steven Box and Chris Hale (1983). In response to an earlier piece of Canadian research, which connected the movement of women out of the family from the early 1930s to the late 1960s with increases in their property crime (Fox and Hartnagel, 1979), Box and Hale attempted a British investigation along similar lines. Focusing on a later period, the early 1950s to the late 1970s, they considered a range of indicators of changes in women's role, from decreasing fertility (number of children) to improvements in higher education. They also examined the costs for women of rising levels of unemployment and endeavoured to correlate all these variations with observed increases in female crimes against property, employing multiple regression analysis. Their key finding was that financial insecurity was the most important variable: 'as women become economically worse off, largely through unemployment and inadequate compensatory levels of welfare benefits, so they are less able and willing to resist the temptations to engage in property offences as a way of helping solve their financial difficulties' (Box and Hale, 1983:199).

An emerging appreciation that women are the main victims of recession and unemployment suggests an obvious line of future inquiry into the causes of female theft. What the Australian social theorist Bettina Cass (1985) calls the 'feminization of poverty', the growth of the female population dependent on welfare benefits, provides a likely explanation of crimes for economic gain.

In her account of the poverty of Australian women, Cass observes, from the outset, that an international comparison of the extent and nature of poverty in six of the countries of the Organisation for Economic Co-operation and Development (including the United Kingdom, the United States and Australia) in the early to mid-1970s identified sex as a key determinant. More specifically, being female and unattached indicated such a profound risk of poverty that it was described as a 'disability'. Remarking that this was the plight of women 'before the depths of recession', Cass proceeds to examine the changes in the situation of Australian women from the early 1970s to the early 1980s.

Cass discovers that one of the principal ways that the position of Australian women has actually deteriorated during the time under study is through the substantial growth of single-parent families headed by women and in receipt of income maintenance:

> Between 1974 and 1982 there was an increase of 68 % in the number of single parents ... but a much greater increase ... in the numbers of single parents where the parent was not employed ... However, the prevalence of mothers as the single parent has barely changed: they were 87% of single parents in 1974, 85% in 1982 (Cass, 1985:78).

With the diminishing employment opportunities of this period, there was an increase in the numbers of both male and female single parents receiving benefits. Nevertheless, 'women remained four times more likely than men to be dependent on social security benefits and in June 1983 accounted for 96% of all single parents in receipt of pension or benefit'. By 1983, the size of the problem was considerable: 'Income units headed by women comprise[d] one quarter of all income units, but one half of income units in poverty.' Cass concludes that both before and after the recession of the mid-1970s, 'women and their children bore a very disproportionate share of poverty' (Cass, 1985:78, 81, 83).

A final challenge to Adler is directed at her claim that women are now using crime as an expression of feminism. The empirical work on the connection between feminist attitudes and criminality not only tends to disprove Adler's thesis but also raises interesting questions about women's role and the meaning of offending.

In an effort to test offenders for feminist sympathies, Gloria Leventhal (1977) administered questionnaires designed to elicit attitudes to women to samples of incarcerated criminal women and college women. The offending group saw women as weak, less capable than men and unable to control their emotions. Tending to perceive themselves as unfeminine, they nevertheless advocated a traditional role for women: they should be submissive and faithful housewives. Queried about their view of the women's liberation movement, most adopted a clearly anti-feminist stance. The responses of the college sample indicated a very different attitude: 'that women should assert themselves, play a leading role where applicable, and maintain their equality in social-sexual matters, employment, education, and family decisions' (Leventhal, 1977:1187).

Attitudes to traditional and non-traditional female roles also formed the focus of an inquiry into the relationship between 'liberation' and delinquency conducted by Giordano and Cernkovich (1979). Employing samples of institutionalised delinquent girls and high-school students, these researchers came to the view that 'there did not appear to be a strong link between liberated attitudes and actual involvement in delinquency'. In fact those correlations which were discovered were either insignificant or in the wrong direction. That is, 'the more "liberated" the response the less delinquent' (Giordano and Cernkovich, 1979:477). Those girls who believed that women should enter the workforce and that a woman's role was not necessarily confined to child-rearer were the least delinquent. A complicating factor, however, was that when asked about their reasons for offending, delinquents tended to give traditionally unfeminine rationalisations—such as 'to compete with men' and 'for the thrill of it'—rather than indicating that theirs was a passive role.

An 'Attitude Toward Women Scale' was administered to a small sample of incarcerated women and their non-criminal controls in Cathy Spatz Widom's investigation into the impact of feminist beliefs on female criminality (Widom, 1979). Again the offenders proved to be significantly less feminist in their attitudes. Suspecting this to be a result of a variance in educational level of offending and non-offending subjects, Widom controlled this variable and managed to eliminate the significant difference between the two groups. She was not able, however, to reverse her results to produce a finding which would accord with the women's liberation thesis.

A questionnaire designed to measure opinions on feminism was employed by James and Thornton (1980) in a further attempt to test the effects of the women's movement on the criminality of women. Delinquent and non-delinquent subjects were drawn from samples of male and female high-school students who were asked to disclose any offences they had committed. Girls who agreed with the aims of the feminist movement were about as delinquent as its detractors, with any differences occurring in the direction opposite to that predicted by the women's liberation thesis. More significantly, girls who reported ample opportunity to offend and strong support for delinquency were less likely to engage in aggressive delinquency when they held attitudes favourable to feminism. The authors inferred from this that 'positive attitudes toward feminism tend to inhibit rather than promote delinquency involvement' (James and Thornton, 1980:240).

Brought together, the results of this research support a case against the usual characterisations of masculinity and femininity and their association with crime. Although female offenders subscribe, in theory, to the traditional version of women's role and nature, the practice is different. Criminal women do not describe themselves as feminine; nor do they give conventional reasons for their offending. On the other hand, females who believe that the sexes are equal and that women should be assertive tend to be law-abiding. Indeed a commitment to feminism is a positive force for conformity when there is opportunity to offend as well as peer-group support for delinquency.

All of these findings contain a challenge to traditional criminology. They suggest that it is wrong to assume that the more an individual adopts the characteristics of the traditional male, in particular his alleged autonomy and audacity, the more likely is that person to offend. They cast doubt on the notion that crime is an expression of liberation and daring (Hagan's view). They reveal also that women are neither thinking nor acting in ways which criminologists have normally assumed. More specifically, the data indicate that criminologists (Adler included) have employed misleading propositions about the so-called 'traditional' and the 'non-traditional' woman. The traditional woman is supposed to be domesticated, passive, dependent and conformist or criminal only in feminine ways. The non-traditional woman is allegedly aggressive, independent and likely to break the law. But the evidence reveals that women do not slot comfortably into such categories. More interestingly, 'feminist' and 'masculine' women show a high degree of commitment to conformity: the literature from the control school suggests that these women value conventional social networks and display concern for their members. This discovery does much to contradict the idea of the passive and compliant conforming female contained in the standard accounts of crime.

The several propositions which have been identified here as the components of the women's liberation thesis have all tended to be disproved by attempts to verify them empirically. Women are not substantially more violent than before the women's movement, although their petty property offending has flourished. Masculinity in women does not appear to be related to criminal propensity, or at least not in the direction predicted by Adler and her followers. The complex hypothesis that white-collar female crime is expanding because of improved occupational opportunities for women is undermined by crime statistics which show that women are still principally shoplifters—not business or white-collar criminals—and by demographic data which indicate that the women's movement has not brought about any significant change in women's occupational mobility. And this is particularly true of the socioeconomic bracket of women who make up the population of offenders. Finally, efforts to uncover the aggressively competitive nature of criminal women looking for their 'piece of the action' or to find signs of feminism among female offenders have met with remarkably little success.

None of this is helpful in explaining, however, why petty property offending has increased over the past few decades. One theory already mentioned is the poor economic position of women. Notwithstanding the suggestions of Adler and Simon that women are moving into male occupations, a brief review of recent labour statistics reveals that women are not only still confined to a narrow range of traditionally female jobs (though the range is greater than before) but that they are experiencing higher rates of unemployment than men.[3] As we saw above, Bettina Cass (1985) presents a strong case for the 'feminization of poverty' in her account of the financial position of Australian women in the 1970s and early 1980s. Economic pressures therefore could be providing the impetus for women to steal from stores.

8

Re-writing the human sciences
The impact of feminism

In a trenchant criticism of traditional epistemology, Catherine A. MacKinnon maintains that a male construction of knowledge is all-pervasive. It so colours our accounts of the world that it is virtually invisible. It appears in the guise of objective truth but conceals a male view. MacKinnon describes as substantial the feminist task of laying bare the foundations of the male orientation to knowledge.

> The perspective from the male standpoint enforces woman's definition, encircles her body, circumlocutes her speech, and describes her life. The male perspective is systematic . . . there is no ungendered reality or ungendered perspective . . . objectivity—the nonsituated universal standpoint, whether claimed or aspired to—is a denial of the existence or potency of sex inequality that tacitly participates in constructing reality from the dominant point of view (MacKinnon, 1982:636).

The agenda for feminism, argues MacKinnon, is 'to uncover and claim as valid the experience of women'. This is an experience which has been submerged and denigrated. The feminist undertaking is also to expose 'the male point of view as fundamental to the male power to create the world in its own image'. Feminism, declares MacKinnon, 'comprehends that what counts as truth is produced in the interest of those with power to shape reality' (MacKinnon, 1982:638, 640).

The project of this book is part of the larger task of feminism. The common purpose is to reveal the male perspective which has constructed accounts of the female in a manner which is not only unfaithful to her experience, but which positively seeks to devalue the 'other' sex. In this chapter, the endeavour will be to show that the treatment of women by the criminologists considered above is congruent with a male world view which informs the human sciences and which feminists have now begun critically to examine. The work of this book shares with the larger feminist undertaking the aim of displaying the sexism of a particular discipline. It does not extend, however, to an explanation of the origins of female stereotypes, an ambitious project attempted by other feminist writers (O'Brien, 1981).

The present inquiry into feminist criticism and the social sciences does not seek to be exhaustive. The limited aim is to demonstrate the pervasiveness of male bias in interpretations of social behaviour which purport to be value-free. The intention is also to show the uniformity across disciplines of an idealised male and of a devalued female. The same set of ennobling male attributes and the same indictment of the female *persona* appear in each area of teaching.

Four fields of feminist social scholarship are considered in this chapter: philosophy, psychology, political science and (industrial) sociology. In each of these disciplines, feminists have taken issue with the orthodox view of social behaviour and identified a masculine bias. Although the feminist works examined here are all notable for their cogency of argument, it would be misleading not to acknowledge the growing body of feminist literature which has begun to question almost every area of Western thought. The following selection from the new feminist canon, with a view to economy of argument, focuses on some key pieces of writing which have posed fundamental challenges to their author's discipline. A fuller treatise would not only include a number of other important writers but would extend analysis across the other disciplines.

The argument of this chapter, then, is that criminologists are at one with scholars in the other human sciences who have been shown to cast men in a dominant and superior role and project onto women those attributes which have been designated inferior, and hence antithetical to the male model. This

chapter will demonstrate that criminologists are already familiar
with these characteristics assigned to men and women because
they are central to their own theorising. Criminology's unequal
evaluation of the sexes, as feminists have revealed across the
disciplines, has a considerable ancestry.

HUMAN NATURE AND THE MAN OF REASON

It is in philosophy that one finds the more extensive feminist
statements on the male version of reality which is thought to
devalue the female. In an early feminist tract *Women and
Philosophy* (1976), Carol Gould showed the way forward by
arguing the sexism of traditional conceptions of human nature.
Gould's contention is that the properties which characterise
the human condition are in fact qualities men have purloined
for themselves. Though said to apply to humanity in general,
they are neither universal nor gender-neutral. The official view
of the essential nature of the human being, declares Gould,
invests it with those qualities 'which the philosophers themselves have either explicitly identified as male properties, or
which [have been] associated with roles and functions in which
males [have] predominated' (Gould, 1976:17). To demonstrate
her point, Gould presents selected extracts from the works of
some major Western philosophers.

In the writing of Kant one finds the paradigmatic sexist
account of human nature. In the following passages we see
Kant associating morality with rationality, declaring that rationality is a quality of the male and then depicting the female in
quite another way. First, Kant tells us,

> [t]hat is practically *good*, however, which determines the will by
> means of the conceptions of reason . . . on principles which are
> valid for every rational being as such. It is distinguished from the
> *pleasant* as that which influences the will only by means of
> sensation from merely subjective causes (Gould, 1976:18).

Kant then explicitly connects his idea of 'good' based on reason
with the male in the statement: 'Now I say: man and generally
any rational being exists as an end in himself.' We discover that
Kant does not intend the word 'man' to be read here in a

generic sense when we turn to his account of women as moral creatures. Simply, they do not possess the most important human quality of reason which forms the basis of all moral agency: 'Women will avoid the wicked not because it is unright, but only because it is ugly . . . Nothing of duty, nothing of compulsion, nothing of obligation! . . . They do something only because it pleases them . . . I hardly believe that the fair sex is capable of principles' (Gould, 1976:18).

It is the German post-Kantian philosopher Schopenhauer, however, who provides Gould with her most striking example of misogynist philosophy on the nature of being human. 'Woman,' according to Schopenhauer, 'is in every respect backward, lacking in reason and reflection . . . a kind of middle step between the child and the man, who is the true human being . . . In the last resort, women exist solely for the propagation of the race' (Gould, 1976:19).

Kant and Schopenhauer are not exceptional in their treatment of the sexes. On the contrary, they illustrate the traditional philosophical approach to men and women. They demonstrate that human nature or essence, 'whether it be construed as freedom or reason or in some other way', is associated with the sex of the individual: 'it is found only or truly in men and not women' (Gould, 1976:20).

A contributor to Gould's edited volume, Lawrence Blum, has since extended the feminist critique of Kant. Blum maintains that the Kantian approach exemplifies a general orientation within moral philosophy, what he terms 'moral rationalism'. 'For the moral rationalist,' says Blum, '*reason* and *rationality* are at the centre of the conception of the good or moral man' (Blum, 1982:287). Equally, they are thought not to be present in the female, who is therefore constitutionally incapable of arriving at a state of moral maturity.

Philosophy's moral man is rational, self-contained, exercises strength of will and acts from universal principles. Importantly for the feminist critique, the moral man is also cool-headed, emotionally distant and uninvolved in matters of the heart. The moral man possesses traits which are archetypally masculine, argues Blum. Such qualities serve him well: they ennoble his experience and present it as a universal state of virtue. The same Kantian philosophy, Blum tells us, downgrades the emotions which are thought to be connected with the female role. Moral rationalism excludes from the concept of the moral person the virtues of 'sympathy, compassion, kindness, caring for others, human concern, emotional responsiveness'. These are considered 'capricious' and 'unreliable' emotions (Blum, 1982:296, 288).

The 'virtues' that Kant is willing to accord the female are poor things by comparison with the qualities of the moral man. Women have 'charm, docility, and obedience'. They are 'passive', 'modest', 'accommodating' and compliant. 'The qualities attributed to women,' according to Blum, 'are either not genuine moral virtues at all, or are ones of minor significance.' Worse still, from the feminist perspective, the qualities which Kant allows the female 'entail a set of virtues which men as the dominant sex find convenient in a lower, subservient class'.

Blum makes several substantial points. Moral philosophy, exemplified by the writing of Kant, presents an interpretation of the moral person which entails the characteristics thought to be found in men, not women. These are autonomy, rationality, strength of will and self-determination. Second, women are explicitly found wanting in these attributes essential to moral maturity. The virtues they are conceded describe a set of devalued, accommodating attributes suitable to an inferior caste. They are not significant virtues. Third, morality as portrayed by Kant is a partial concept: it excludes the emotions. To Blum, kindness and compassion should play a central role in conceptions of moral maturity: 'not only our actions but our emotional reactions have moral significance.' These are virtues which have conventionally been identified with the female role, 'for women are generally expected to be [and seen as] more emotional, emotionally expressive and emotionally responsive than are men'. But in philosophical accounts of moral maturity these human aspects have been repudiated. Philosophy has preferred to see the female in terms of an associated but reduced set of virtues: compassion becomes compliance in the female; kindness and care become a willingness to submit to male authority (Blum, 1982:289, 295).

A more ambitious historical review of philosophical

approaches to reason and morality has been undertaken by
Genevieve Lloyd (1983). She contends that the idea of
women's inferior capacity to reason goes back to the Greeks.
From the time of Plato, Western thought has advanced different
and unequal models of the sexes. Lloyd cites the Greek philosopher Philo, who declared that the male was 'active, rational,
incorporeal and more akin to mind and thought'. The female, by
contrast, was described in terms of the baser senses rather than
the intellect. Closer to nature than the male, she was 'material,
passive, corporeal and sense-perceptible' (Lloyd, 1983:491,
495, 494).

A salient theme in early Western philosophy, attests Lloyd,
was the perception of woman as symbolically nearer than man
to the 'entanglements' of sense and matter. She was bound up
with nature and its reproduction. The man was accorded the
more significant intellectual functions. The effect was to assign
woman a secondary and derivative status. The paradigm of
rational excellence was male. The female's exclusive function
was helpmate to the male who embodied the human qualities.
The ideal of the rational was 'genderised': it assumed a male
subject.

The tendency to define moral maturity in terms of pure
intellect or the capacity to reason was strengthened with the
rise of Cartesian logic. Descartes' proposition that true knowledge of the world stems from pure thought, dissociated from
the body, was explicitly applied to the male only. The woman
was relegated to the sphere of the sensuous: 'To be truly
rational, he must leave soft emotions and sensuousness behind;
she will keep them intact for him' (Lloyd, 1983:508).

The late eighteenth and early nineteenth century saw a
further development in the male conception of reason. The
view became entrenched that pure, rational thought provided
the basis of the morally mature decision and that it was only the
male who was capable of these cerebral processes. To soften
the blow to women, however, a new idea was fostered, that of
the complementary nature of the sexes. Women, it was now
said, had a different kind of understanding. They possessed 'taste,
sensibility, practical sense, feeling' (Lloyd, 1983:510). Lloyd is
with Blum in maintaining that this elevation of the female was

spurious. It was a ploy to denigrate women by assigning them an inferior set of characteristics. The male was still taken to be the norm, the human standard. His qualities were preferred to those of the female.

While Kant was positively chivalrous in his devaluation of women—learning detracts from their 'beautiful understanding' of the world—other nineteenth-century philosophers were more candid. In his essay *On Women*, Schopenhauer described women's inability to reason as a form of immaturity. Women attained a 'very limited sort' of reason so that they remained 'big children, their whole lives long'. Hegel in *The Philosophy of Right* was equally explicit in deriding the female:

> Women regulate their actions not by the demands of universality but by arbitrary inclinations and opinions. Women are educated—who knows how?—as it were by breathing in ideas, by living rather than acquiring knowledge. The status of manhood, on the other hand, is attained only by the stress of thought and much technical exertion (Lloyd, 1983:511).

Lloyd's account of the misogynist underpinnings of Western philosophy is important for current feminist theory. It explains the provenance of a powerful male bias in such contemporary categories as 'reason' and 'morality'. There is a firm historical basis, Lloyd informs us, for the present practice of depicting human excellence in terms of a male norm. A direct line of descent from the Greeks to modern philosophy ensures that it is still only the male who is deemed capable of disembodied thought, the highest human process. This intellectual inheritance is also the reason for modern presentations of women as the complementary sex, purveyors of the passions.

In a second collection of feminist philosophical papers edited by Carol Gould in 1983, the critique of male bias has been taken a step further. The aim of this recent work has been not only to reveal the gendered nature of philosophy but also to reformulate some of the central concepts to accommodate the female experience. Perhaps the most challenging stand taken against the discipline in this volume is that of Sandra Harding (1983) in a paper entitled 'Is Gender a Variable in Conceptions of Rationality? A Survey of Issues'.

Harding's point of departure is the proposition that feminists have now established the sexism of philosophy. The work has been done by writers such as Blum and Lloyd. It is now plain that

> [f]rom antiquity to the present day, women have been claimed less capable of abstract and systematic thought than men, less capable of developing a mature sense of justice than men, more ruled by the emotions, the passions and the appetites than men, and more inclined toward subjective assessments and less toward objective ones than men (Harding, 1983:43).

Harding approves the findings of her feminist colleagues that the history of Western thought is in fact the history of Western man. It is therefore the history of a distinctive social experience of the world. The important consequence for women is that philosophy's depiction of the female has been consistently distorted. 'The distinctively masculine perspective' which has been presented as 'human rationality' is not only one-sided but perverse. Harding reasons that because men are the dominant sex, their interests rule the lives of women. It follows that men not only have limited insights into the nature of the female experience but that their understanding is shaped by the master–slave relationship.

At this stage in her argument, Harding is simply elaborating the case made by writers such as Blum about the sexism of Kant and his successors. Harding maintains that the characteristics imposed on women by philosophy suit men, the dominant class. The female, accordingly, is deemed compliant, passive and docile. The ascription to women of such a malleable disposition not only makes life more comfortable for men but also serves to devalue the subordinate caste.

It is in her endeavour to articulate a specifically female concept of rationality that Harding moves beyond feminist criticism and begins to refashion philosophy. Her stated aim is to develop an account of reason which is based on the life of the female, not the male. This is not simply a matter of adding women as objects of knowledge to the current range of philosophical concepts. This would not work, she says, because the existing references to women in philosophy are not just meagre but positively misleading. 'The prevailing theories . . . draw on and legitimate a [male] conceptual screen that systematically distorts our vision of women and their lives' (Harding, 1983:46). So philosophy must be rewritten from a new viewpoint, the perspective of the female. Harding undertakes to illuminate the distinctive experiences of women and then connect those experiences with a female construction of reason.

Harding makes herself controversial by approving the argument of feminist psychologist, Nancy Chodorow (1978), that the lives of women differ in vital respects from the lives of men. Male development, Harding claims, depends on mothers perceiving their sons as unlike themselves and therefore fostering their separation and individuation. Boys are encouraged thus to see themselves as autonomous and independent. Female development, by contrast, entails continuity in the relationship with the mother, mothers and daughters perceiving themselves as kindred spirits. The girl matures, therefore, through a process of attachment rather than differentiation.

The different developments of the sexes are said to have powerful effects on the adult male and female. For men, as we have seen, 'a rational person values highly his ability to separate from others and to make decisions independent of what others think—to develop "autonomy"'. The rational person from the female perspective is quite another being. She 'values highly her abilities to empathise and "connect" with particular others and wants to learn more complex and satisfying ways to take the role of the particular other in relationships'. It is this 'relational rationality' of the female that has been depicted by traditional philosophy as 'immature' and 'subhuman' (Harding, 1983:53).

Harding's interpretation of the different natures of the sexes has its feminist detractors. Genevieve Lloyd, for one, feels that it is dangerous for feminists to subscribe to theories of the sexes which underline the sort of differences which have been used to devalue women. The ascription to women of well-developed powers of empathy is closely connected with the traditional view that women have baser natures because they are closer to the passions (Lloyd, 1984:106). This objection notwithstanding, Harding's account of female reason is strengthened by association with a new feminist psychology whose exponents have sought to confirm empirically the existence of a female 'voice'. The key figure in the feminist revision of developmental psychology is the American moral psychologist Carol Gilligan (1982). Her proposition is that women speak with a different and distinctive moral language which is of at least equal value to the male voice but which, until now, has been devalued by a male-biased psychology.

MORAL MATURITY AND THE FEMALE VOICE

In the same manner as her feminist colleagues in philosophy, Carol Gilligan maintains that a partial perspective informs accounts of human development in her own discipline, psychology. The perspective is that of the male. Gilligan observes that across the social sciences, 'theories formerly considered to be sexually neutral in their scientific objectivity are [being] found instead to reflect a consistent observational and evaluative bias'. It is with the world viewed through 'man's eyes that the categories of knowledge' have been constructed. Psychologists are guilty of the same bias. 'Implicitly adopting a male life as the norm, they have tried to fashion women out of masculine cloth' (Gilligan, 1982:6).

To illustrate the masculinity of the paradigm that has shaped psychology, Gilligan takes her analysis back to Freud, 'who built his theory of psychosexual development around the experiences of the male child that culminate in the Oedipus complex'. The autonomy of the female child and the configuration of her family relationships are aberrant, according to Freud. The extent to which the female differs from the male is the extent of her deviation from the model of healthy human development. Difference from the male means maladjustment. One result is that women 'show less sense of justice than men . . . that they are more often influenced in their judgements by feelings of affection or hostility' (Gilligan, 1982:6, 7).

Freud's approach to women has determined the course taken by psychology in its treatment of the sexes, suggests Gilligan. Psychologists have followed Freud's lead in blaming women, not their own theories, for the dissonance observed between their models of development (based on the male) and the maturation of women. Rather than question their own accounts of psychological growth, members of the discipline have persisted in finding women wanting. 'Thus a problem in theory [has been] cast as a problem in women's development, and the problem in women's development [has been] located in their experience of relationships' (Gilligan, 1982:7). Gilligan's assertion is that, in the tradition of Freud, psychologists of the twentieth century have come to equate the development of the child with male development and to deride women for their failure to fit the model.

Prominent members of her discipline still equate humanity with masculinity, maintains Gilligan. Jean Piaget (1965), who considers children's games to be 'the crucible of social development during the school years', finds girls more tolerant than boys in their attitude toward rules: they regard 'a rule as good as long as the game repays it'. Boys, on the other hand, develop an increasing fascination 'with the legal elaboration of rules and the development of fair procedures for adjudicating conflicts'. Piaget's reaction to the differences he observes between the sexes is to conclude that 'the legal sense', which he considers essential to moral development, is 'far less developed in little girls than in boys' (Gilligan, 1982:10).

Erik Erikson (1950) has charted eight stages of psychological development which describe a process of individuation. Maturity, in Erikson's scheme, involves autonomy, initiative and industry. These are the qualities that individuals acquire if they are unimpeded in their psychological growth and blossom into successful adults. But women, as Erikson admits, do not fit this pattern. Instead, the female comes to know herself through her relationships with others, not through the processes of detachment. Erikson infers from this that the female process of maturation is at fault: females do not develop into mature, autonomous adults.

Lawrence Kohlberg (1981) has also documented stages of human development, focusing on the emergence of the attributes of autonomy, impartiality and objectivity. Again, women are found deficient according to the dominant paradigm. They reach only the third stage of development, the halfway point. They remain sensitive to the needs of particular others. They fail to develop a concern for abstract, impersonal and universal rights—Kohlberg's sixth and final stage of maturity. Kohlberg does not respond to this finding by modifying his theory to fit the female case. Instead, he falls in with his colleagues and suggests that the problem is with women: that they are simply immature.

From her observations about contemporary psychology and its treatment of the sexes, Gilligan concludes that her discipline sees the world as male. Women are regularly cast in the role of 'other' than the man. It follows that when female behaviour does not accord with the male standard—derived from men's observations of men—it is assumed automatically that there is something wrong with women, not with the psychological model.

Gilligan does more than challenge the masculinity underpinning supposedly gender-neutral theories of human development. She offers also her own interpretation of the nature of female maturation which seeks to value rather than to denigrate women. Gilligan's argument is the same as that advanced by Harding. With women cast in the role of principal child-rearers, girls do develop differently from boys, but not in an inferior manner as psychologists have maintained. The close association between mothers and daughters, the mother's sense of her daughter being like herself, fosters in the girl a sense of connection rather than separation. The girl's formative experience is one of continuity in relationships, of attachment and identification with others. The boy's experience is the opposite. The mother perceives him as unlike herself so that maturity for the boy is cast in terms of separation and individuation. The result is an adult female who defines her relationships in terms of mutual dependence and attachment and an adult male who values individuality and differentiation. But as Gilligan observes, it is only the male style which one finds in the psychological tests of development and which is esteemed by the discipline.

The failure of psychological theories to acknowledge the female mode of development means that they harbour a fatal flaw, in Gilligan's view. Psychological models 'reflect a conception of adulthood that is itself out of balance, favouring the separation of the individual self over connection to others, and leaning more toward an autonomous life of work than toward the interdependence of love and care'. Gilligan believes that if psychologists were to undertake research with the female rather than the male as central subject, they would derive ideas of human development quite unlike those of Piaget, Erikson and Kohlberg. Key moral issues would concern instead 'conflicting responsibilities' rather than 'competing rights'. The dominant style of thinking would also differ; it would be 'contextual and narrative rather than formal and abstract' (Gilligan, 1982:17, 19).

Gilligan's account of the moral development of men and women suggests that there are two opposing ethical styles. The male approach she calls an 'ethic of rights'. The female mode she dubs an 'ethic of responsibility'. The rights style, which is manifest in Kohlberg's stages of human development, devalues the female approach. In fact it treats most adult women as only half-formed. At Kohlberg's third stage, morality 'is conceived in interpersonal terms and goodness is equated with helping and pleasing others' (Gilligan, 1982:18). It is men who progress to the higher stages, with their 'rights' style of thinking. The morally mature male subordinates particular relationships to universal principles. He values his independence and autonomy. He is a man of action and initiative who functions best in glorious isolation. He spurns the more personal priorities of the female.

To verify her theory of a specifically female moral 'voice', Gilligan constructed an experiment around the moral problem of the decision to abort a pregnancy. She reasoned that when a woman considers this issue 'she contemplates a decision that affects both self and others and engages directly the critical moral issue of hurting'. The aim of the study was to discover how a group of women dealt with a major moral choice. More particularly, Gilligan sought to determine whether her subjects employed an ethics of responsibility. The sample comprised 29 women 'ranging in age from 15 to 33 and diverse in ethnic background and social class' who were referred to the study by an abortion counselling service (Gilligan, 1982:71). The research method entailed two interviews of each subject: one at the time they were making the decision and another at the end of the following year.

The interviews were conducted in two stages. In the initial phase, the women were asked for their thoughts on the decision they confronted: 'how they were dealing with it, the alternatives they were considering, their reasons both for and against each option, the people involved, the conflicts entailed, and the ways in which making this decision affected their views of themselves and their relationships with others.' The second stage of the interview was of a less specific nature. The women were asked to consider how they would resolve three hypothetical moral dilemmas. Considered together, the two interviews were intended to produce information of a very general sort about how women think about problems in their lives rather than revealing what women feel about the 'abortion choice' (Gilligan, 1982:72).

The evidence yielded by the study tended to confirm the theory that there is a distinctively female moral voice. Gilligan found her subjects employed a language of altruism. With great regularity, they defined their moral problem as 'one of obligation to exercise care and avoid hurt'. Their central concern was the welfare of others, rather than the competing rights of individuals. Their overarching moral requirement was to be kind and to refrain from causing injury. 'The moral imperative that emerges repeatedly in interviews with women is an injunction to care, a responsibility to discern and alleviate the "real and recognisable trouble" of this world' (Gilligan, 1982: 73, 100).

Gilligan's disquisition on the female 'ethic of care' has generated much debate. She has been criticised on several counts. There is the objection, also levelled at Harding, to the treatment of women's compassion as their strength. It is said to be dangerously close to the traditional view of the sexes—that men think and women feel (Lloyd, 1983). The collection of virtues identified by Gilligan in women have been described as failing to provide a clear guide to ethical living; an undifferentiated ethic of care is thought to justify any action (Walker, 1983; Broughton, 1983). Gilligan has also been accused of a tendency to essentialise gender, to make her female qualities seem timeless, because she fails to locate her analysis historically (Code, 1983).

Despite substantial and perhaps justified opposition to Gilligan's idea of the compassionate female (which also has its supporters, witness Harding), her critique of her discipline stands as a powerful indictment of psychology's gendered thinking and male bias. Gilligan has argued convincingly that psychology supports as human a collection of values traditionally associated with masculinity. The question she poses for all of the human sciences is whether these values should be accepted uncritically. Gilligan's own response is in the negative. She can see no reason why autonomy should be esteemed while altruism is denigrated.

THE UNPOLITICAL FEMALE

The feminist enterprise of uncovering the gender bias in social theory extends also to the political sciences. 'That politics is a man's world is a familiar adage,' claim Susan L. Bourque and Jean Grossholtz (1984). Less accepted, they suggest, is the notion that 'political science as a discipline tends to keep it that way'. Bourque and Grossholtz advance two propositions about their discipline: politics employs a sexual definition and political science perpetuates it. In the choice of data to be analysed, as well as in their interpretation, 'the discipline insists upon a narrow and exclusive definition of politics which limits political activity to a set of roles which are in this society, and many others, stereotyped as male'. The tendency in political theory, as in the other social sciences, is to find the standard of appropriate behaviour in the male and to regard women as aberrant and therefore at fault in some important dimension. Bourque and Grossholtz cite approvingly Bella Abzug who suggests that 'what is really ludicrous is a political structure that denies representation to a majority of its population and then winds up fingering the victims of this situation as somehow responsible for it because of their personal inadequacies' (Bourque and Grossholtz, 1974:225).

The method chosen by Bourque and Grossholtz to evaluate

their discipline is a review of some of the classic works of political science to discern their view of women. They also cast a critical eye over the most recent publications to see whether there has been a continuity of perspective. The evidence thus yielded on the official treatment of the political woman is then organised into four broad statements about political writing, past and present.

The first challenge levelled at political scientists is that they 'fudge' their footnotes. They ascribe to women certain political characteristics which are not substantiated by the material they produce as their source of evidence. Political researchers abuse the data they derive from earlier investigations by discarding the cautious language of the original empiricists and by disregarding qualifications to data. The result is either the distortion or the falsification of results.

'The assumption of male dominance' is the second disclosure of this study. It entails an expectation among political scientists that men will dominate the political arena, a finding that this is so, but then a failure to consider why. Political scientists, declare Bourque and Grossholtz, are unconcerned about the implications of their discovery that it is men who occupy public office and who control political decisions. Instead of scholarly inquiry into the reasons for male political dominance, writers in the field simply assert and accept this to be the natural state of affairs. It is taken to be a reflection of the ascendancy of men and the subservience of women in family life; the natural order is that of the dominating male breadwinner and his dependent wife. From this, political theorists extrapolate, without furnishing the necessary evidence, that men control women even when women are engaged in decisions of a non-familial nature. 'For example, women's political attitudes are assumed to be reflections of those of the father or husband.' But this condemns women on two counts. It suggests not only that women are poorly represented in public decisions but that it is their own fault: 'it is women's preferences which give men control of politics' (Bourque and Grossholtz, 1974:228). With male dominance thus established, women who are conspicuous in public roles are duly ignored by the literature. The paradigm stands of the influential political animal as male.

A third manner in which political writing has distorted the position of the female is in its portrayal of 'masculinity as ideal political behaviour'. With neither explanation nor examination, theorists have employed conventional depictions of masculinity to describe effective political activity. The ideal political person, say Bourque and Grossholtz, displays the stereotypically male characteristics and values of aggressiveness, competitiveness and pragmatism. The obverse is also true. Political decisions are deemed irrational when they are influenced by the qualities associated with women, in particular their supposed subjectivity and emotionalism.

Finally, political scientists are said to display a 'commitment to the eternal feminine'. They assume a powerful connection between the political behaviour of women and women's social role of wife and mother with 'her mythical status of purity personified'. Women's inferior political standing is thought to be both necessary and functional. For women to operate effectively in their domestic capacity, as relaxed and loving wives and mothers, they must be buffered from the corrupting and exhausting demands of political life.

Bourque and Grossholtz published their challenge to political science in 1974. More recent feminist criticism suggests that the discipline has not since revised its approach to women in the light of their findings. Janet Siltanen and Michelle Stanworth, in their assessment of the material in *Women and the Public Sphere* (1984), indicate that a decade on, the profession's idea of the political woman remains unaltered. Their survey of the literature on electoral and work-based politics discloses 'in both areas a conception of politics, and of sophisticated political activity, that devalues the political experience of women and privileges that of men' (Siltanen and Stanworth, 1984:9). Political analysis, they contend, persists with its insensitivity to gender.

Siltanen and Stanworth derive a number of propositions from their political review. All speak of the denigration of women. 'First, women are held to participate in politics less frequently, less forcefully, and less readily than men' (Siltanen and Stanworth, 1984:11). Women are to be found on the margins of the political sphere. Relative to men, they are seen as politically apathetic, inactive and uninvolved.

'Second, where women's participation is acknowledged, it is commonly held to be less sophisticated, and in many cases less authentically *political*, than the involvements of men.' Women are swayed by the personal qualities of candidates when it comes to voting. Hence they fail to respond to the relevant political issues. At times it is said that women 'personalise' politics, draining it of its real political content. Siltanen and Stanworth observe also that women in electoral politics are assumed to 'echo mindlessly' the preferences of their husbands. This amplifies further the sense of women as incapable of genuine political activity. 'Unsophisticated levels of political understanding are alleged to underlie women's political choices, and their supposedly lower levels of "conceptualisation" give rise to the occasional inference that, in effect, women do not know what they are talking about' (Siltanen and Stanworth, 1984:12, 12).

A third objection to political science made by Siltanen and Stanworth concerns its reduction of the aims of women to a narrow set of conventionally feminine issues. Where women are discerned to be actively involved in political matters, they are described as morally rather than politically engaged. This tendency to deny the political acumen of women, and to attribute their political involvement to a form of private morality rather than to public interest, is most marked in political analyses of attitudes to war. Siltanen and Stanworth observe that 'the greater enthusiasm of men and boys for war is designated political, and taken as an index of political awareness, while the comparatively strong objections of girls and women to war are designated "moral"'. The net effect is that the different approaches of the sexes to war are taken as evidence of the superior politicisation of the male.

A final criticism of political writing offered by Siltanen and Stanworth is directed at the discipline's portrayal of women as more conservative than men. Evidence to the contrary, they say, has not retarded the frequency of claims that women are electorally conservative. A powerful stereotype of the conformist female prevails over the various indications in the empirical literature that women are not acting according to type.

Siltanen and Stanworth believe their findings reveal the

dominance of a 'male-stream analysis' in political science. The representation of women's political behaviour as 'marginal, shallow or conservative' derives from an intellectual tradition which, both theoretically and empirically, assumes a male experience. That is to say, what is political is what men do; what women do is something else again.

The parallels between the images of men and women in political science and those of the sister disciplines of philosophy and psychology are plain. Uniformly, the message is that males provide the measure of suitable behaviour: the temperament of the male is ideal and the female is deficient in most essential respects. In political science, as in the associated disciplines, 'sexual stereotypes have relegated most women to the status of camp followers and the rest to the status of deviants, while at the same time convincing men that by virtue of their masculinity they have real participation' (Bourque and Grossholtz, 1974:264).

WOMEN AS WORKERS

A final example of feminist dissatisfaction with social scholarship, which confirms the prevalence of sexual stereotyping, comes from industrial sociology. 'It is one of those taken-for-granted assumptions,' says Kate Purcell (1984), 'that women, and particularly women workers, are generally more placid, stable, fundamentally exploitable than men.' She cites a recent publication on industrial disruption to open her case. According to C. Northcote Parkinson, industrial peace is to be found in those trades where women predominate because women are 'more concerned about their children's welfare than about loyalty to a trade union or to the working class'. Purcell maintains that 'a passive woman worker thesis' is central to the sociological writing on workers. Sociologists sustain this idea in several ways. They remark on the political invisibility of women in the workplace. They draw on the psychological literature which endeavours to demonstrate that men are aggressive, competitive and independent, while women are careful and conventional. And they employ a basic premise that the main job of women is that of wife and mother. From this it is assumed to follow that women are less committed to work, that they are more privatised, less universal in their thinking 'and essentially a reactionary brake to working-class revolutionary zeal'. Sociologists operate on the assumption that the occupational dichotomy of male-breadwinner and female-homemaker is a part of the natural order and any deviation from it flies in the face of nature (Purcell, 1984:54, 56).

While Purcell concentrated her efforts on the specific industrial issue of militancy, Roslyn Feldberg and Evelyn Nakano Glenn (1984) have taken a broader view and have brought their feminism to bear on the sociology of work as a whole. Their principal claim is what we have now identified to be the standard feminist objection to social science: that male bias poses as gender-neutrality. 'While issues of work are framed as universal ones,' say Feldberg and Glenn, 'the actual study of work has proceeded along sex-differentiated lines.' Masculine bias in the sociological literature on work generates a number of problems. One is the omission of women from research. Work studies tend to choose for their subjects white males. A second problem is that the analysis of findings derived from the few studies of women is sex-biased. Finally, the discipline's entire approach to work is distorted by sexist assumptions that certain factors are relevant only to women and others only to men.

From their review of the industrial sociological material, Feldberg and Glenn decide that two quite different models guide research: according to the sex under investigation, sociologists select either a 'job' or 'gender' approach. The 'job' model has been applied to men, the 'gender' model to women. Simply, this means that when sociologists consider men as workers, they look at work conditions and their effect on the worker. The male worker is the paradigm; the terms 'worker' and 'male' are virtually synonymous. When sociologists address the woman as worker, however, they do not consider her work; instead, they look at her gender, or more specifically, her family role of wife and mother. Feldberg and Glenn suggest that the basis of this different treatment of the sexes is the dichotomy of male-worker and female-wife which emerged with the separation of public and private spheres during the industrial revolution. Since this moment in history, any differences observed by industrial sociologists between men and women have been attributed to this polarisation of sexual function. Even when women are employed, their public work role has been deemed secondary to their more authentic family function.

The import of these models for those who conduct research into the work of men and women is that they filter and distort evidence. If the subject is male, sociologists assume that both behaviour and attitudes to work are the result of experiences in the work-place. If the worker is female, responses are considered an outcome of experiences within the family. Feldberg and Glenn employ two major studies of the sexes at work— Blauner's (1964) inquiry into the textile industry and an investigation of production-line workers conducted by Beynon and Blackburn (1972)—to support this claim. Here they find clear signs of a shaping of the evidence, with behaviour which does not fit the gender stereotypes set aside and identical behaviour in the sexes explained differently—according to the models. They remark also on the tendency to regard male responses as 'normal' and women's responses as 'variants'.

THE CHALLENGE OF GOOD SCHOLARSHIP

Feminists writing about philosophy, psychology, political science and sociology have argued the existence of a male bias which takes the same form as the skewed thinking of criminologists. Each discipline uses categories organised around gender, though they are presented as universal in their application. Supposedly gender-free norms of behaviour on closer scrutiny reveal the normal person to be male. Feminists have also suggested that the normal male is not presented 'warts and all'; instead, he is a romantic illusion. The idealised man of the social sciences is by now a familiar figure: he was present in each of the critiques of criminology contained in earlier chapters. That man is autonomous, unemotional, objective, rational, active, assertive, self-determining, competitive and achieving. This cluster of values suits contemporary capitalist society, to a high degree, though the deep historic roots of the male ideal demonstrated by Genevieve Lloyd suggest that its purpose is other than the validation of the existing economic system. They suggest, instead, that the characterisation of the male depends on the complexion of the age. Men are described according to the qualities valued in any given period. The consistent depiction of males as autonomous, rational and objective can be attributed to a remarkable continuity in the idealisation of these qualities, going back to the Greeks.

The value of juxtaposing the various feminist accounts of academic social theory lies in the disclosure that across the disciplines there is a high degree of similarity in descriptions of men. As we shift from philosophy to psychology, from the political sciences to industrial sociology, and finally to criminology, there persists a unitary construct of the male. The idealised man revealed by philosophers—the dispassionate man of reason—is closely related to political man: the hard-headed decision-maker. Independence, intelligence, and objectivity are the key characteristics of academe's social man. Whatever males do, whether they are exemplifying human nature, being morally mature, assuming the role of political animal or the role of worker, or being criminal, they are depicted in just these terms.

With the same regularity, the norm of human behaviour across the social sciences has been found to exclude those qualities thought to be associated with the female. Moreover, those attributes which are said to be feminine have been consistently devalued. There is a uniform, unflattering depiction of women in all the academic fields considered. Woman is 'other', she is 'not the norm', she is dependent, emotional, subjective, irrational, passive, determined, uncompetitive, unachieving, immature and unintelligent. Whatever women do, they are described thus. In criminological circles, where the standard of behaviour is that of the criminal male, the more law-abiding female is still depicted as an aberration. This has the curious result of extolling the virtues of the male, as a good criminal, and treating conforming women as if they were the socially deviant group. Even when women are right, it seems they are still wrong.

In certain disciplines, the task of exhibiting the sexism of social scholarship has gone beyond simple demonstrations of discrimination against women. Feminists such as Sandra Harding in philosophy and Carol Gilligan in psychology have begun to rethink and to reconstruct the basic categories and concepts. In doing so they have sought to redress the balance, to expound the female experience, and thus to give women a voice.

The import of feminism and its critique of the human sciences for criminology lies in this revelation that the orientation of criminologists is but a small part of a longstanding tradition of male bias in Western thought. The endeavour of previous chapters to lay bare the gendered theories and methods of criminologists was a contribution to this larger feminist project of reconstructing knowledge so that it no longer reflects exclusively a male social reality.

In sum, criminology has been faithful to a high degree to the standard academic view of the male disclosed by feminists. Consistently, it has taken positions which assume that the behaviour of the male is normal, while the female is deviant. It has glamorised the male through portrayals of daring, aggressive and imaginative offenders. It has stigmatised the conforming female, describing her as weak, passive and dependent. It has insisted on using gendered models of behaviour which can now be seen to be drawn directly from more established disciplines.

9

A feminist agenda
for criminology

The task of this final chapter is to move beyond the stage of feminist criticism of the discipline and to map a plan for a new feminist criminology. With the nature and provenance of sexism in the discipline now understood, the problem remains of what to do with women. The job is made easier by the fact that much is already known about the subject. Criminologists operating from the various perspectives considered in this volume have done a good deal of work on the female offender, even though their most interesting findings have been obscured by gendered thinking. If we now return to the criminological writing on women, sensitive to the distortions of sexual stereotypes, a number of avenues of investigation become apparent.

The empirical literature suggests that frustration is associated with crime. Albert Cohen's theory of female strain was misleading to the extent that it imposed on women a limited set of sexual concerns, without bothering to verify them. Research has since revealed that females are susceptible to frustrations of a more general nature and that these frustrations correlate positively with their offending. However, Cohen's original account of the sexes, of the delinquent boy with his occupational frustrations and of the sexually frustrated delinquent female, has yet to be substantially modified. At the head of the feminist agenda for strain theory is the investigation of the concerns, the goals and the frustrations of criminal and conforming women. The existing criminological evidence suggests that women are not acting according to type. They are expressing concern about issues which are not traditionally associated with the female role. And yet they are not driven to offend in anything like the numbers of males. Strain theory, in its original version, is unable to cope with these findings. Feminists should endeavour to resolve the dilemma posed by the evidence by eliciting from their subjects their own accounts of their frustrations and their impact on their behaviour.

Criminologists seeking to test the theory of differential association with women have also found their subject not conforming to their expectations. They have had more success at locating girls who act like boys, in responding to encouragement to offend, than at demonstrating the existence of the passive and cloistered female, insulated from criminal influences. But differential association holds promise as a theory of female offending precisely because females do appear to respond to the criminal urgings of their friends, and particularly to the encouragement of girlfriends. Girls, like boys, find the courage to offend when they are placed in a milieu which supports delinquency, and that milieu may entail a group of girls who favour offending. Sutherland did not anticipate findings such as these. Criminologists since Sutherland who are now the wiser—they know that girls do behave in non-traditional ways—have failed to modify the original formulation. Feminist criminologists need to investigate the criminal subcultures of girls. Differential association may well prove a valuable intellectual tool when it comes to explaining the transmission of delinquent attitudes between girls and their consequent offending. As an Australian criminologist has recently observed about the current state of research in this area, so far we 'have only scratched the surface' (Alder, 1985:62).

There is another strand of differential association theory which feminist criminologists might find useful when applied to the law-abiding behaviour of women. In his exposition of the theory, Sutherland spoke of altruistic cultures in which cooperation and care were considered more important than the priorities of the individual. Such societies tended to be peace-loving, said Sutherland, because there was a high level of concern for one's fellow citizens. Sutherland did not employ this thinking to explain the conformity of women in modern industrial societies which were supposed to foster criminal tendencies. Instead of pursuing the idea of an altruistic female culture, Sutherland maintained that what he termed the greater 'niceness' of women was simply a product of socialisation into anti-criminal patterns. Feminists might consider the possibilities of a theory of female conformity along the lines of Sutherland's altruistic culture. Carol Gilligan has already suggested that there is a distinctively female voice which employs an ethic of care. A new book by Nel Noddings (1984) entitled *Caring* explores similar ideas. It may be that the 'ethic of care' can be put to further work as an explanation of the lesser criminality of women in a manner already hinted at by Sutherland.

Feminists who wish to revive the masculinity theory of crime will have to negotiate the same problems which confronted their colleagues in the 'strain' school. Parsons assumed a set of interests and concerns in women which have yet to be tested by criminologists. The empirical work on masculinity theory since Parsons suggests that his account of the sexes is no longer (if it ever was) accurate. Feminists who intend to pursue the theory that either offending or conforming in women is an expression of traditional gender roles, be they masculine or feminine, must first determine how women see those roles and their degree of fit with their own lives. We know already that there are no clear correlations between femininity and conformity, nor between masculinity and offending. High masculinity in females certainly is not a good predictor of offending. As women assume masculine characteristics, their propensity to offend does not appear to increase. If anything, the opposite is true. Feminist criminologists would be wise to consider the meaning of the basic working models, masculinity and femininity. They should examine the extent to which men and women do in fact display these gendered characteristics, an issue which continues to exercise mainstream psychology (Sonderegger, 1985). And they should address the nature of the connection between such gendered personalities and offending. The body of data with which they start their inquiries suggests a need to rethink the fundamental categories. Feminists may find that their task is to forge an entirely new set of connections between gender, personality and crime, one which repudiates the traditional Parsonian distinction between the aggressively masculine offending male and the pliant and passively conforming female.

An unexpected set of findings yielded by criminologists in the control school perhaps offers the most interesting line of inquiry for feminist criminologists. Thornton and James, and Shover and his associates discovered that their 'masculine' females were conventional in their attachments (they cared about their conventional relationships) and that this appeared to inhibit their offending. This disclosure throws into doubt the orthodox view, put forward by control theorists such as John Hagan, that it is the stereotypically female qualities (passivity, compliance, dependence) which bond women to the conventional order. It hints at a different interpretation of female conformity, one which is perfectly consistent with Hirschi's founding theory of control as applied to men, but which is almost revolutionary in its implications when women become the subjects of analysis. It is revolutionary because it shatters the still dominant stereotype of the law-abiding woman. This alternative approach has much in common with Carol Gilligan's theory of a female ethical voice, but implies an even more powerful female persona. The new idea for feminism is that law-abiding women are not vapid, biddable creatures, clinging helplessly to conventional society. Instead, they are, to use Hirschi's description of conforming men, responsible, hardworking, engrossed in conventional activities and people and perfectly rational in their calculation not to place all this at risk by engaging in crime.

If we take as our paradigm case of the conforming woman the housewife and mother who also juggles a paying job, the new characterisation makes a lot of sense—in fact more sense than Hirschi made with his conforming male. Our paradigmatic woman is certainly involved and engrossed in conventional life; indeed she is run off her feet. But she is also actively concerned about the effects of her behaviour on her loved ones, particularly emotionally and financially dependent children.

Her greater involvement (than the father) in the nurturing of her children provides her with a more powerful attachment to the conventional order. The injunction to be responsible, to be an upright citizen, is strong.

That such a woman bears little relation to the passive female stereotype of criminology is suggested by some of the 'liberation' literature. Criminologists who have sought to test Adler's theory of an association between being liberated and the propensity to offend have found that Adler was wholly wrong. The more 'liberated' the woman, the more feminist her attitudes, the less she is likely to offend. James and Thornton are unambiguous about their finding that 'positive attitudes toward feminism tend to inhibit rather than promote delinquency involvement'. Now if we consider this result in conjunction with the material that shows that masculine women demonstrate a high degree of commitment to conventional relationships, the type of conforming woman who exemplifies the ethic of care may indeed be a stout character. She may believe in the equality of the sexes, she may be strong and assertive, but she may nevertheless take seriously her social duties. What appeared to Adler to be an obvious reaction to independence, women testing the criminal waters, becomes an irrational act to the woman who is conscious of her place in a network of social responsibilities.

One problem with this account of the conforming woman is that it is likely to generate the same objections as those levelled at Carol Gilligan. It may be imprudent for feminist criminologists to imply that the very qualities which have traditionally been linked with women's oppression, in particular their compassion, have the positive effect of making women good citizens. From here it is but a short step to the anti-feminist proposition that women should be encouraged to shoulder their current load of responsibilities because it keeps them out of trouble.

A more important problem with the proposed Gilligan-style of feminist criminology is an insufficient empirical base. Though it is tempting to celebrate women's difference, to say that women care more than men about people and therefore tend not to offend, as yet we do not know why women act as they do. There is no good, non-sexist scholarship which demonstrates that the greater conformity of women is a function of their special virtues. The existing literature is only suggestive.

The type of empirical work which would give women a voice in criminology has already been pioneered by criminologists in the 1960s researching the deviant male. Employing the techniques of participant observation, thereby developing an affinity with his subject, Howard Becker presented convincing and sympathetic portraits of his fellow jazz musicians. It is likely that the same approach would produce important insights into the lives of women. Carol Gilligan's own work makes powerful reading, in the same way as Becker's *Outsiders*, because she allows her subjects to speak, at length, for themselves. Such detailed and time-consuming ethnographic research is likely also to bear fruit for feminist criminologists.

Considered as a whole, the agenda for feminist criminology is to demonstrate to the more traditional members of the discipline that the conventional view of women is inaccurate. Women are to be observed behaving in ways which do not fit the theories, but it is women, not the theories which have been found deficient. There exists in the present body of evidence a more positive construction of women which must no longer be obscured. The task of feminists is to see that this more active and interesting woman is given a voice, that her experiences are rendered faithfully and incorporated into criminology.

The new feminist criminology is therefore poised to challenge the discipline's most fundamental categories. In its refusal to accept the values, the experiences and the behaviour of the male as the standard, as the norm, it promises to transform the entire field of scholarship. Feminist theory is likely to dismantle the longstanding dichotomy of the devilish and daring criminal man and the unappealing and inert conforming woman. The threat it poses to a masculine criminology is therefore considerable.

Notes

Chapter 1 The reasonable man

1   The other offence category in which women feature in large numbers, and indeed are the principle offenders, is that of prostitution. It would be wrong, however, to take the crime statistics on prostitution as evidence of a specifically female tendency to sell sexual favours. Instead, the official data need to be interpreted in the light of legal definitions of the crime and legal practice. Although English law recognises that members of either sex can be prostitutes, Carol Smart maintains that 'the category of "offence by prostitute" in the Official Statistics relates only to women; men are not charged with this, which in fact refers mainly to soliciting' (Smart, 1976:6). The crime figures, according to Smart, therefore give a false impression that prostitutes are inevitably female. In the United States, legal definition rather than practice dictates the female nature of prostitution. Although the law varies from State to State, the crime of prostitution is often described as 'the practice of a female offering her body to an indiscriminate intercourse with men, usually for hire' (Hoffman-Bustamante, 1973:119).

2   There is now a substantial literature addressed to the treatment of females by the juvenile justice system. It has revealed consistently that girls are penalised more than boys for sexual transgressions (see Chesney-Lind, 1974; Fielding, 1977; Omodei, 1981; Hancock, 1980; Hiller, 1982).

3   This debate is elaborated in Chapter 6 within the context of a discussion of the effects of the women's liberation movement on the offending of women.

4   The criminological tendency to depict male delinquency as heroic has also been observed in a recent text by Frances Heidensohn (1985:Chapter 7). She affirms Millman's point that the sociology of deviance has consistently celebrated the young male delinquent, treating females as peripheral to analysis.

5   A Marxist approach is not included in this volume for the simple reason that the Left has shown little specific interest in the female offender. In the mid-1970s, there were rallying calls about the need to revitalise the

study of female crime within a radical critique of society (Klein and Kress, 1976; Smart, 1976). Unfortunately they have yet to generate a recognisably Marxist account of the subject (Rafter and Natalizia, 1981; Rafter, 1986). A recent entreaty to her colleagues by one Marxist criminologist, to the effect that women would be best served by the development of ideologically sound crime-control strategies, suggests that writers on the Left may now have decided to subordinate the theoretical branch of the criminology of women to more practical concerns (Rafter, 1986).

Chapter 3 Learning crime

1   See Campbell (1976), Jamison (1977), Shacklady Smith (1978) and Mawby (1980) for the results of studies conducted in the United Kingdom, and Weis (1976), Cernkovich and Giordano (1979) and Richards (1981) for research into self-reported offending conducted in the United States of America.

Chapter 4 Masculinity theory

1   More recent attempts to bring the literature on female crime together and apply a critical approach to the theory have not advanced significantly the state of the art. Although Eileen Leonard's *Women, Crime and Society* (1982) is an interesting attempt to apply to women the standard crime theories, she does not claim to break any new intellectual ground. Likewise, Frances Heidensohn's (1985) synthesis of the literature provides a valuable introduction to the study of women and crime but does not profess to develop new theory. She remains squarely within the control school in her own account of women's offending.

Chapter 6 Crime and stigma

1   A recent study of socially-disadvantaged girls in New South Wales provides a good example of the sort of work which might be done with the adult female offender. By way of detailed interviews, the subjects of this inquiry were encouraged to describe their experiences of a broad range of social problems. The authors state explicitly that their intention was 'to give the girls a voice and to outline what girls in care and girls at risk see as their issues and concerns' (Women's Co-ordination Unit, 1986:30).

Pat Carlen's *Criminal Women* (1985) provides a further example of research which presents the female subject's own view. The four short autobiographies which comprise this volume allow the women in question to offer their own interpretations of their actions. The result, as the author observes, is that we are allowed to see the rationality and coherence of purpose which inhere in female criminal conduct (Carlen, 1985:8).

Chapter 7 The women's liberation thesis

1   Data from the Women's Bureau, Department of Employment and Youth Affairs (1981:2) indicate that women are still employed in large numbers in the clerical (32.4 per cent), sales (13.1 per cent), and service (16.9 per cent) areas.

2   See Barron and Norris, 1976 (cited by Smart, 1979) for a discussion of the worsening economic position of women.
3   Statistics from the Women's Bureau, Department of Employment and Youth Affairs (1981:29) reveal that in 1979 approximately 5 per cent of males and 8 per cent of females were unemployed in Australia.

Bibliography

Adler, F. (1975) *Sisters in Crime: The Rise of the New Female Criminal* New York: McGraw Hill

Alder, Christine (1985) 'Theories of female delinquency' in Allan Borowski and James M. Murray (eds) *Juvenile Delinquency in Australia* Melbourne: Methuen, p. 54.

Anyon, Jean (1983) 'Intersections of gender and class: accommodation and resistance by working-class and affluent females to contradictory sex-role ideologies' in Lea Boston and Stephen Walker (eds) *Gender, Class and Education* Sussex: Falman Press

Baker, David (1985) *Introduction to Torts* Sydney: The Law Book Co.

Balkan, S. and R.J. Berger (1979) 'The Changing Nature of Female Delinquency' in C.B. Kopp (ed.) *Becoming Female: Perspectives on Development* New York and London: Plenum Press, p. 207

Becker, H.S. (1963) *Outsiders: Studies in the Sociology of Deviance* New York: Free Press.

Bertrand, M.A. (1969) 'Self Image and Delinquency: A Contribution to the Study of Female Criminality and Woman's Image' *Acta Criminologica* p. 71

Beynon, H. and R.M. Blackburn (1972) *Perceptions of Work* Cambridge: Cambridge University Press

Blauner, R. (1964) *Alienation and Freedom* Chicago: University of Chicago Press

Blum, L.A. (1982) 'Kant's and Hegel's Moral Rationalism: A Feminist Perspective' *Canadian Journal of Philosophy* 12, 2, p. 287

Bourque, Susan C. and Jean Grossholtz (1974) 'Politics an Unnatural Practice: Political Science Looks at Female Participation' *Politics and Society* Winter, p. 225

Box, S. (1981) *Deviance, Reality and Society* London: Holt, Rinehart & Winston
—— (1983) *Power, Crime and Mystification* London: Tavistock

Box, S. and C. Hale (1983) 'Liberation and Female Criminality in England and Wales' *British Journal of Criminology* 23, 1, p. 35

Brady, J.F. and J.G. Mitchell (1971) 'Shoplifting in Melbourne' *Australian and New Zealand Journal of Criminology* 4, 3, p. 154

Brittan, Arthur and Mary Maynard (1984) *Sexism, Racism and Oppression* Oxford: Basil Blackwell

Broughton, J.M. (1983) 'Women's Rationality and Men's Virtues: A Critique of Gender Dualism in Gilligan's Theory of Moral Development' *Social Research* 50, 3, p. 597

Cameron, M.O. (1964) *The Booster and the Snitch* New York: Free Press of Glencoe

Campbell, A. 1981 *Girl Delinquents* Oxford: Basil Blackwell

Carlen, P. (1985) *Criminal Women* Oxford: Polity Press

Cass, B. (1985) 'The Changing Face of Poverty in Australia: 1972–1982' *Australian Feminist Studies* 1, p. 67

Cernovich, S.A. and P.C. Giordano (1979) 'A Comparative Analysis of Male and Female Delinquency' *Sociological Quarterly* 20, p. 131

Chapman, J.R. (1980) *Economic Realities and the Female Offender* Lexington, Mass.: Lexington Books

Chesney-Lind, M. (1974) 'Juvenile Delinquency: The Sexualisation of Female Crime' *Psychology Today* July, p. 44

—— (1979) 'Chivalry Re-examined: Women and the Criminal Justice System' in L.H. Bowker (ed.) *Women, Crime and the Criminal Justice System* Lexington, Mass.: Lexington Books, p. 197

Child, I.L., E.H. Potter and E.M. Levine (1946) 'Children's Textbooks and Personality Development: An Exploration in the Social Psychology of Education' *Psychological Monographs* 60, 3, p. 35

Chodorow, Nancy (1978) *The Reproduction of Mothering* Berkeley: University of California Press

Clark, S.M. (1964) 'Similarities in Components of Female and Male Delinquency: Implications for Sex-Role Theory' in W.C. Reckless and C.L. Newman (eds) *Interdisciplinary Problems in Criminology: Papers of the American Society of Criminology* Columbus Ohio State University, College of Commerce and Administration, p. 217.

Cloward, R. and L. Ohlin (1960) *Delinquency and Opportunity: A Theory of Delinquent Gangs* New York: Free Press

Code, L.B. (1983) 'Responsibility and the Epistemic Community: Woman's Place' *Social Research* 50, 3, p. 537

Cohen, A.L. (1955) *Delinquent Boys: The Culture of the Gang* New York: Free Press

Constantinople, A. (1973) 'Masculinity-Femininity: An Exception to a Famous Dictum' *Psychological Bulletin* 80, 5, p. 389

Crites, L. (1976) 'Women Offenders: Myth vs. Reality' in L. Crites (ed.) *The Female Offender* Lexington, Mass.: Lexington Books

Cullen, F.T., K.M. Golden and J.B. Cullen (1979) 'Sex and Delinquency: A Partial Test of the Masculinity Hypothesis' *Criminology* 17, 3, p. 301

Curran, D.A. (1983) 'Judicial Discretion and Defendant's Sex' *Criminology* 21, 1, p. 41

Datesman, S.K., F.R. Scarpitti and R.H. Stephenson (1975) 'Female Delinquency: An Application of Self and Opportunity Theories' *Journal of Research in Crime and Delinquency* 12, July, p. 107

Durkheim, E. (1951) *Suicide* trans, J.A. Spaulding and G. Simpson, New York: Free Press

Edwards, A.R. (1983) 'Sex Roles: A Problem for Sociology and for Women' *Australian and New Zealand Journal of Sociology* 19, 3, p. 385

Edwards, S.M. (1984) *Women on Trial: A study of the female suspect, defendant and offender in the criminal law and criminal justice system* Manchester: Manchester University Press

Eichler, M. (1980) *The Double Standard: A Feminist Critique of Feminist Social Science* London: Croom Helm

Erikson, Erik, H. (1950) *Childhood and Society* New York: W.W. Norton

Farrington, D.P. and A.M. Morris (1983) 'Sex, Sentencing and Reconviction' *British Journal of Criminology* 23, 3, p. 229

Feldberg, Roslyn and Evelyn Nakano Glenn (1984) 'Male and Female: job versus gender models in the sociology of work' in J. Siltanen and M. Stanworth *Women and the Public Sphere* London: Hutchinson p. 23

Fielding, J. (1977) 'Female Delinquency' in P. Wilson (ed.) *Delinquency in Australia: A Critical Appraisal* Queensland: Queensland University Press, p. 153

Fox, G.L. (1977) '"Nice Girl": Social Control of Women through a Value Construct' *Signs* 2, p. 805

Fox, J. and T.F. Hartnagel (1979) 'Changing Social Roles and Female Crime in Canada: A Time Series Analysis' *Canadian Review of Sociology and Anthropology* 16, 1, p. 96

Gilligan, C. (1982) *In a Different Voice: Psychological Theory and Women's Development* Cambridge: Harvard University Press

Giordano P. (1978) 'Research Note: Girls, Guys and Gangs: The Changing Social Context of Female Delinquency' *Journal of Criminal Law and Criminology* 69, 1, p. 126

Giordano, P.C. and S.A. Cernkovich (1979) 'On Complicating the Relationship between Liberation and Delinquency' *Social Problems* 26, 4, p. 467

Gould, C.C. (1976) *Women and Philosophy: Toward a Theory of Liberation* New York: G.P. Putnam's

—— (1983) 'Private Rights and Public Virtues: Women, the Family and Democracy' in C.C. Gould *Beyond Domination: New Perspectives on Women and Philosophy* New Jersey: Rowman & Allanheld, p. 3

Green, E. (1961) *Judicial Attitudes in Sentencing* London: Macmillan

Grosser, G.H. (1951) Juvenile Delinquency and Contemporary American Sex Roles, PhD thesis, Harvard University

Hagan, J., J.H. Simpson and A.R. Gillis (1979) 'The Sexual Stratification of Social Control: A Gender-Based Perspective on Crime and Delinquency' *British Journal of Sociology* 30, p. 25

Hall, S. and P. Scraton (1981) 'Law, Class and Control' in M. Fitzgerald, G. McLennan and J. Pawson (eds) *Crime and Society: Readings in History and Theory* London: Routledge & Kegan Paul, p. 460

Hancock, L. (1980) 'The Myth that Females are Treated More Leniently than Males in the Juvenile Justice System' *Australian and New Zealand Journal of Sociology* 16, 3, p. 4

Harding, Sandra (1983) 'Is Gender a Variable in Conceptions of Rationality? A Survey of Issues' in Gould *Beyond Domination* p. 43

Harris, A. (1977) 'Sex and Theories of Deviance: Toward A Functional Theory of Deviant Type-Scripts' *American Sociological Review* 42, p. 3

Heidensohn, F. (1968) 'The Deviance of Women: A Critique and an Enquiry' *British Journal of Sociology* 19, 2, p. 160

—— (1985) *Women and Crime* London: Macmillan

Hiller, A.E. (1982) 'Women, Crime and Criminal Justice: the State of

Current Theory and Research in Australia and New Zealand' *Australian and New Zealand Journal of Criminology* 15, p. 69

Hindelang, M.J. (1973) 'Causes of Delinquency: A Partial Replication and Extension' *Social Problems* 20, 4, p. 471

Hirschi, T. (1969) *Causes of Delinquency* Berkeley: University of California Press

Hoffman Bustamante, D. (1973) 'The Nature of Female Criminality' *Issues in Criminology* 8, 2, p. 117

James, J. and W. Thornton (1980) 'Women's Liberation and the Female Delinquent' *Journal of Research in Crime and Delinquency* 17, 2, p. 230

Jamison, R.N. (1977) Personality, Anti-Social Behaviour and Risk Perception in Adolescents, paper delivered to the British Psychological Society, London, 1971. Cited in Campbell (1981:23)

Jensen, G.J. and R. Eve (1976) 'Sex Differences in Delinquency: An Examination of Popular Explanations' *Criminology* 13, p. 179

Klein, D. (1973) 'The Etiology of Female Crime: A Review of the Literature' *Issues in Criminology* 8, 2, p. 3

Klein, D. and J. Kress (1976) 'Any Woman's Blues: A Critical Overview of Women, Crime and the Criminal Justice System' *Crime and Social Justice* 5, p. 34

Kohlberg, Lawrence (1981) *The Philosophy of Moral Development* San Francisco: Harper & Row

Kohlberg, L. and C. Gilligan (1971) 'The Adolescent as Philosopher: The Discovery of the Self in a Post Conventional World' *Daedalus* 100, 4, p. 1051

Leonard, E.B. (1982) *Women, Crime and Society: A Critique of Theoretical Criminology* New York and London: Longman

Levanthal, G. (1977) 'Female Criminality: Is "Women's Lib." to Blame?' *Psychological Reports* 41, p. 1179

Lloyd, G. (1983) 'Reason, Gender and Morality in the History of Philosophy' *Social Research* 50, 3, p. 490

—— (1984) *The Man of Reason: 'Male' and 'Female' in Western Philosophy* London: Methuen

Lombroso, C. and W. Ferrero (1985) *The Female Offender* London: Fisher Unwin

Loy, P. and S. Norland (1981) 'Gender Covergence and Delinquency' *The Sociological Quarterly* 22, p. 275

Mawby, R. (1980) 'Sex and Crime: the Results of a Self-Report Study' *British Journal of Sociology* 31, 4, p. 525

Mackinnon, Catherine (1982) 'Feminism, Marxism, Method, and the State: An Agenda for Theory' *Signs* 7, 3, p. 515

McRobbie, A. (1982) book reviews: A. Morris *Women and Crime*; C.T. Griffiths and M. Nance *The Female Offender*; A. Campbell *Girl Delinquents* in *International Journal of Sociology of Law* 10, p. 217

Merton, R.L. (1949) *Social Theory and Social Structure* New York: Free Press

Miller, E.M. (1983) 'International Trends in the Study of Female Criminality: An Essay Review' *Contemporary Crisis* 7, p. 59

Millman, M. (1975) '"She Did It All For Love": A Feminist View of the Sociology of Deviance' in M. Millman and R. Moss Kanter (eds) *Another Voice* New York: Anchor Books, p. 251

Morris, R. (1964) Female Delinquency and Relational Problems *Social Forces* 43, p. 82

—— (1965) 'Attitudes toward Delinquency by Delinquents, Non-Delinquents and their Friends' *British Journal of Criminology* 5, p. 249

Mukherjee, S.K. and R.W. Fitzgerald (1981) 'The Myth of Rising Female Crime' in Mukherjee and Scutt (eds) *Women and Crime* p. 127

Mukherjee, S.K. and J.A. Scutt (eds) (1981) *Women and Crime* Sydney: Australian Institute of Criminology with Allen & Unwin

Mukherjee, S.K., E.N. Jacobsen and J.R. Walker (1981) *Source Book of Australian Criminal and Social Statistics 1900–1980* Canberra: Australian Institute of Criminology

Muncie, J. and M. Fitzgerald (1981) 'Humanising the Deviant: Affinity and Affiliation Theories' in M. Fitzgerald, G. McLennan and J. Pawson (eds) *Crime and Society: Readings in History and Theory* London: Routledge & Kegan Paul, p. 403

Naffin, N. (1983) Criminality, Deviance and Conformity in Women, PhD thesis, University of Adelaide

Noddings, Nel (1984) *Caring: A Feminine Approach to Ethics and Moral Education* Berkeley: University of California Press

Norland, S., R.C. Wessel and N. Shover (1981) 'Masculinity and Delinquency' *Criminology* 19, 3, p. 421

O'Brien, Mary (1981) *Politics of Reproduction* Boston: Routledge & Kegan Paul

Omodei, R. (1981) 'The Myth Interpretation of Female Crime' in Mukherjee and Scutt *Women and Crime* p. 51

Owen, M. and S. Shaw (1979) *Working Women: Discussion Papers from the Working Women's Centre, Melbourne* Carlton, South Victoria: Sisters Publishing

Parisi, N. (1982) 'Are Females Treated Differently? A Review of the Theories and Evidence on Sentencing and Parole Decisions' in N.H. Rafter and E.A. Stanko (1982) *Judge, Lawyer, Victim, Thief: Women, Gender Roles and Criminal Justice* Northwestern University, p. 205

Parsons, T. (1954) *Essays in Sociological Theory* rev. edn, Glencoe, Illinois: Free Press

Pateman, C. (1980) '"The Disorder of Women": Women, Love and the Sense of Justice' *Ethics* 91, p. 20

Piaget, Jean (1965) *The Moral Judgement of the Child* New York: The Free Press

Piven, F.F. (1981) 'Deviant Behavior and the Remaking of the World' *Social Problems* 28, 5, p. 490

Price, R.R. (1977) 'The Forgotten Female Offender' *Crime and Delinquency* 23, 2, p. 101

Purcell, Kate (1984) 'Militancy and Acquiescence among Male Workers' in Siltanen and Stanworth *Women and the Public Sphere* p. 54

Rafter, N.H. (1986) 'Left Out by the Left: Crime and Crime Control' *Socialist Review* 89, p. 7

Rafter, N.H. and E.M. Natalizia (1981) 'Marxist Feminism: Implications for Criminal Justice' *Crime and Delinquency* 27, p. 81

Richards, J.R. (1980) *The Sceptical Feminist: A Philosophical Enquiry* Harmondsworth: Penguin

Richards, P. (1981) 'Quantitative and Qualitative Sex Differences in Middle-Class Delinquency' *Criminology*, 18, 4, p. 453

Rogers, W.V.H. (1984) *Winfield and Jolowitz on Tort* London: Sweet & Maxwell

Rozenkrantz, P., S. Vogel, H. Bee, I. Broverman and D.M. Broverman (1968) 'Sex Role Stereotypes and Self Concepts in College Students' *Journal of Consulting and Clinical Psychology* 32, p. 287

Scutt, J.A. (1978a) 'Toward the Liberation of the Female Lawbreaker' *International Journal of Criminology and Penology* 6, p. 5

—— (1978b) 'Debunking the Theory of the Female "Masked Criminal"' *Australian and New Zealand Journal of Criminology* 11, p. 23

Shacklady Smith, L. (1978) 'Sexist Assumptions and Female Delinquency: An Empirical Investigation' in C. Smart and B. Smart (eds) *Women, Sexuality and Social Control* London: Routledge & Kegan Paul, p. 74

Shover, N., S. Norland, J. James, and W. Thornton (1979) 'Gender Roles and Delinquency' *Social Forces* 58, p. 162

Siltanen J. and M. Stanworth (1984) *Women and the Public Sphere* London: Hutchinson

Silverman, I.J. and S. Dinitz (1974) 'Compulsive Masculinity and Delinquency: An Empirical Investigation' *Criminology* 11, p. 498

Simon, R.J., (1975) *Women and Crime* Lexington, Mass.: Lexington Books

Simons, R.L., M.G. Miller and S.M. Aigner (1980) 'Contemporary Theories of Deviance and Female Delinquency: An Empirical Test' *Journal of Research in Crime and Delinquency* 17, p. 42

Smart, C. (1976) *Women, Crime and Criminology: A Feminist Critique* London: Routledge & Kegan Paul

—— (1979) 'The New Female Criminal: Reality or Myth?' *British Journal of Criminology* 19, p. 50

Smith, D.A. (1979) 'Sex and Deviance: An Assessment of Major Sociological Variables' *Sociological Quarterly* 20, p. 183

Smith, D.A. and C.A. Visher (1980) 'Sex and Involvement in Deviance/ Crime. A Quantitative Review of the Empirical Literature' *American Sociological Review* 45, p. 691

Sonderegger, Theo B. (1985) *Psychology and Gender* Lincoln: Nebraska Press

Steffensmeier, D.J. (1978) 'Crime and the Contemporary Woman: An Analysis of Changing Levels of Female Property Crime, 1960–1975' *Social Forces* 57, 1–2, p. 566

—— (1982) 'Trends in Female Crime: It's Still a Man's World' in B.R. Price and N.J. Sokoloff (eds) *The Criminal Justice System and Women* New York: Clark Broadman, p. 117

Steffensmeier, D.J. and M.J. Cobb (1981) 'Sex Differences in Urban Arrest Patterns, 1934–79' *Social Problems* 29, 1, p. 37

Steffensmeier, D.J. and J.H. Kramer (1980) 'The Differential Impact of Criminal Stigmatization on Male and Female Felons' *Sex Roles* 6, 1, p. 1

Steffensmeier, D. and R.H. Steffensmeier (1980) 'Trends in Female Delinquency: An Examination of Arrest, Juvenile Court, Self Report and Field Data *Criminology* 18, p. 62

Sutherland, E. (1939) *Principles of Criminology* 3rd edn, Philadelphia: Lippincott

Sutherland, E. and D.R. Cressey (1966) *Principles of Criminology* Philadelphia: Lippincott

Thornton, W.E. and J. James (1979) 'Masculinity and Delinquency Revisited' *British Journal of Criminology* 19, 3, p. 225

Tresemer, D. (1975) 'Assumptions Made About Gender Roles' in M. Millman and R. Kanter (eds) *Another Voice: Feminist Perspectives on Social Life and Social Science* New York: Anchor Books, p. 308

Vischer, C.A. (1983) 'Gender, Police Arrest Decisions, and Notions of Chivalry' *Criminology* 21, 1, p. 5

Walker, J. (1983) 'In a Diffident Voice: A Cryptoseparatist Analysis of Female Moral Development' *Social Research* 50, 3, p. 665

Wallace, M. (1981) Is Criminology Helping Women? Notes on the Literature, paper presented at the 51st ANZAAS Conference, Brisbane

Weis, J. (1976) 'Liberation and Crime: The Invention of the New Female Criminal' *Crime and Social Justice* 6, p. 17

Widom, C.S. (1979) 'Female Offenders: Three Assumptions About Self-Esteem, Sex Role Identity and Feminism' *Criminal Justice and Behaviour* 6, 5, p. 365

Women's Bureau, Department of Employment and Youth Affairs (1981) *Facts on Women at Work in Australia, 1980* Canberra: Australian Government Publishing Service

Women's Co-ordination Unit (1986) *Girls at Risk* Sydney: New South Wales Premier's Department

Index

Adler, Freda, 89
Aigner, S.M., 21, 39
Allen, Donald, 17–19
altruism, 31, 41–2, 118–19, 129
American culture, 10–11, 28
anomie, 8, 17, 65
Anyon, Jean, 63, 87
approval of crime, 32–4, 36–7
Becker, Howard, 76–9, 82–3, 133
Bem Inventory, 52, 57–8
Bertrand, Marie Andrée, 48
black offenders, 90
Blum, Lawrence, 108–9
Bourke, Susan L., 119–21
Box, Steven, 60, 64–5, 99
Brittan, Arthur, 63
burglary, 92
Carlen, Pat, 135
Cass, Bettina, 100, 104
Cernkovich, S.A., 20, 101
Chapman, Jane Roberts, 97
chivalry thesis, 1–2
Chodorow, Nancy, 113
Clark, Shirley Merritt, 34, 39
Cloward, Richard, 14–16
Cohen, Albert, 9–25 passim, 28–9, 47, 67, 91, 128

compulsive masculinity, 46, 51, 59
Constantinople, Ann, 60
control theory, 64–75, 131
crime statistics, 1, 92; Home Office, 92; problems with, 92; U.C.R. 92–3
Crites, Laura, 93, 96
Cullen, F.T., 51
Cullen, J.B., 51
cult of the individual, 10, 28–32
Datesman, S.K., 18
delinquent gang, 9, 28
delinquent subculture, 15, 21, 26–42 passim
demographic characteristics, 96
deviant type-scripts, 80–1, 83–4, 87
differential opportunity thesis, 15
differential association, 26–42, 129
Dinitz, S., 51
drug-takers, 89
Durkheim, Emile, 8, 65
economic theory, 99–101, 104
egoism, 29–31, 41
epistemology, 105

Erikson, Erik, 115
Eve, Raymond, 70
Feldberg, Roslyn, 124–5
female stereotype, 59
feminization of poverty, 100–1, 104
feminism, 105; attitudes towards, 101–3, 132; and industrial sociology, 105, 123–5; and philosophy, 105–114; and political science, 105, 119–123; and psychology, 105, 114–19
feminist criminology, 128–33
fertility, 99
Freud, Sigmund, 114–15
gender roles, 43–63 passim
Glenn, Evelyn Nakano, 124–5
Gilligan, Carol, 114–19, 127, 131–3
Gillis, A.R., 68
Giordano, Peggy, 20, 36–7, 101
Golden, K.M., 51
good-girl construct, 81, 87
Gould, Carol, 107–9, 111
Grosser, George, 47
Grossholtz, Jean, 119–21
Hagan, John, 68–70, 81–2, 85, 131
Hale, Chris, 99
Harding, Sandra, 111–14, 127
Harris, Anthony, 80
Hegel, George, 111
Heidensohn, Frances, 134–5
Hindelang, Michael J., 35, 70
Hirschi, Travis, 64–71, 131
Hoffman Bustamante, Dale, 48, 134
human nature, 107
James, Jennifer, 53–4, 71–2, 74, 102, 131–2
Jenson, Gary, 70
juvenile justice system, 134
Kant, Immanuel, 107–9, 111
Klein, Dorie, 48–50, 86

Kohlberg, Lawrence, 115–17
Kramer, John, 82, 85
Kress, June, 48–50, 86
labelling theory, 76–88 passim
labour force participation, 94, 97–9
learning theory, 26–42 passim
Leonard, Eileen, 135
Levanthal, Gloria, 101
Lloyd, Genevieve, 110–13, 125
Loy, Pamela, 55, 73–4
MacKinnon, Catherine A., 105
manslaughter, negligent, 93
Marxist theory, 134–5
masculinity, 9, 13; theory, 43–63 passim, 91, 96, 130
Mawby, Robert, 22, 71
Merton, Robert, 8–9
Miller, M.G., 21, 39
Millman, Marcia, 4–5, 134
moral rationalism, 108–9
Morris, Ruth, 15–17, 19, 32, 39
murder, 93
new female criminal, the, 89–92, 98
Noddings, Nel, 130
Norland, Stephen, 53, 55–8, 72–4
normative conflict, 28
Ohlin, Lloyd, 14–16
opportunity index, 18–19
    educational, 20–1
    illegitimate, 21–2, 90
    occupational, 20–1, 93
    relational, 16, 22
Parsons, Talcott, 43–7, 51, 54, 59, 67, 130–1
participant observation, 77, 79, 87, 133
Piaget, Jean, 115
property crime, 2, 86, 93–5, 104
prostitution, 49, 89, 134
Purcell, Kate, 123–4
reaction formation, 54, 59

reason, 107–14
reasonable man, the, 3–4
robbery, 92
Sandhu, Harjit, 17–19
Schopenhauer, Arthur, 108, 111
Scutt, Jocelynne, 26, 61
self-report studies, 18, 34, 38, 54, 135
sexual delinquency, 13, 16, 19, 40, 48
shoplifting, 1, 36, 40, 49–50, 96, 98
Shover, Neal, 53, 71–4, 131
Simon, Rita James, 93–7
Simons, R.L., 21, 39
Simpson, J.H., 68
Siltanen, Janet, 121–3
Silverman, I.J., 51
single-parent families, 100
Smart, Carol, 36, 49–50, 86, 92, 98, 134

Smith, Douglas, 20, 38, 70–1
social bond theory, 70–71
socialisation, 43–8
Stanworth, Michelle, 121–3
Steffensmeier, D.J., 82, 85, 97
strain theory, 8–25, 128–9
Sutherland, Edwin, 26–42 passim, 67, 91, 129–30
Thornton, William, 53–4, 71–2, 74, 102, 131–2
unemployment, 98–100, 136
violent crime, 89, 92–7
virtue, 45–6
Weis, Joseph, 22
Wessel, R.C., 72
Western culture, 46
white-collar crime, 90, 96
Widom, Cathy Spatz, 52, 102
women's liberation theory, 89–104 passim

Other titles related to women's studies:

Caring for Australia's Children: Political and Industrial Issues in Child Care   Brennan & O'Donnell

Colonial Woman: The Life and Times of Mary Braidwood Mowle   Clarke

Contemporary Feminist Thought   Eisenstein

Ethnicity, Class and Gender   Bottomley & de Lepervanche

Feminist Challenges   Pateman & Gross

The Force of the Feminine: Women, Men and the Church   Franklin

Gender and Power   Connell

Gender at Work   Game & Pringle

Getting Equal: Labour Market Regulation and Women's Work   O'Donnell & Hall

Good and Mad Women: The Historical Construction of Femininity in Twentieth Century Australia   Matthews

Program for Change: Affirmative Action in Australia   Sawer

Subordination: Feminism and Social Theory   Burton

Women, Social Science and Public Policy   Goodnow & Pateman